THE THREE METER ZONE

THE THREE METER ZONE
COMMON SENSE LEADERSHIP FOR NCOs

JAMES D. PENDRY

PRESIDIO

)rinted 2000

Copyright © 1999 by James D. Pendry

Published by Presidio Press, Inc.
505 B San Marin Drive, Suite 160
Novato, CA 94945-1340

Library of Congress Cataloging-in-Publication Data

Pendry, J. D. (James D.)
    The three meter zone : common sense leadership for
NCOs / [J. D. Pendry].
        p.   cm.
    ISBN: 0-89141-679-X (hardcover)
    ISBN: 0-89141-728-1 (paperback)
        1. United States. Army—Non commissioned officers' handbooks. 2. Command of troops. 3. Leadership. I. Title. II. Title: 3 meter zone.
U123.P46   1999
355.3'38—dc21   98-46937
                                                          CIP

Printed in the United States of America

CONTENTS

ACKNOWLEDGMENTS

He has shown you, O man, what is good; And what does the lord require of you but to do justly, to love mercy, and to walk humbly with your God. —*Micah 6-8*

To the following few soldiers and many others who saw fit to share their three-meter zones with me and teach me the real meaning of hard work, high personal values, and dedication, I humbly dedicate *The Three-Meter Zone:*

First Sergeant Pedro Olivari, Sgt. Maj. James White, Capt. Frank Santangelo, Lt. Col. Francis "X" Krahe, Cmd. Sgt. Maj. Lyle Wells, 1st Sgt. Doug Warman, Sgt. Maj. Jim Gorski, Sgt. Rosalie Tapia, Cmd. Sgt. Maj. Bob Halpin, Cmd. Sgt. Maj. Benito Garza, Cmd. Sgt. Maj. Ken Allen, Cmd. Sgt. Maj. Ned Deveraux, Sgt. Maj. Ron Prevost, Col. Gerald Thompson, Cmd. Sgt. Maj. Arthur "Buck" Jones, Sgt. Maj. Antonio Alviar, Cmd. Sgt. Maj. Terry Lovelace, Sgt. Maj. Bob West, Col. Joe Lane, Lt. Col. Greg Evenstad, Lt. Col. Tom Kroeger, Sgt. Shedrick Davis, Cpl. Oren Spears, Sfc. Marsha "Action" Jackson, SSgt. Alicia Clarke, MSgt. Robbie Clarke, SSgt. Ricky Oxyer, SSgt. Connie Harsh, SSgt. Constance Craft, SSgt. David Fortune, SSgt. Al Burger, Specialist Kenneth Blackburn, Sfc. George Jackson, MSgt. Richard Lee, SSgt. Dorman Lloyd, Cmd. Sgt. Maj. David Ahlansberg, Sgt. Maj. Dave Pickerill, Sfc. Hazel Spivey, 1st Sgt. Jeff Patterson, Sgt. Maj. Dub Adkins, Sfc. Yong K. Park, Cmd. Sgt. Maj. James Barrett, 1st Sgt. Larry Southerland, Sfc. Lucy Valdes, Sfc. Clinton Foster, SSgt. Paul Schneidmill, SSgt. Gwen Linder, SSgt. Marcus Campbell, SPC Harry Dudley, Cmd. Sgt. Maj. Sam Goodwin,

ACKNOWLEDGMENTS

Cmd. Sgt. Maj. Ed Johnson, Col. Wayne Ruthven, Ms. M. Carolyn Smith, Ms. Nancy Tennis, Mr. Kim Holien, Sgt. Maj. (Ret.) Don Young, Pvt. James D. Pendry Jr., S1c Hudson Grey Pendry, and all the great soldiers who made me successful. Special thanks for their advice and assistance on this project to SMA Bob Hall, CSM John Leonard, CSM Jack Rucynski, SGM Dan Elder, CSM (Ret) Larry Pence, CSM (Ret) Jimmie Spencer, and CSM (Ret) Randy Mix. And especially my most important combat buddy, critic, and faithful supporter: my wife, Su.

FOREWORD

Command Sergeant Major Dave Pendry in his excellent book, *The Three-Meter Zone,* is doing what noncommissioned officers have been doing forever: teaching, coaching, and mentoring soldiers and other noncommissioned officers. What sets this book apart is that we are provided the opportunity to "sit in" on a counseling session. This makes us all beneficiaries of Cmd. Sgt. Maj. Pendry's wisdom.

All readers, soldiers, NCOs and officers, are getting advice from their units' senior NCO, with no appointment necessary. This counseling session is conducted in a non-threatening environment and absolutely off the record: it gets no better than this.

The Three-Meter Zone doesn't hesitate to expose common lapses in judgment among NCOs. Pendry gives us examples of what we do correctly, while balancing these with other examples of what not to do. Whether or not we agree with his views, his words are always thought provoking.

Command Sergeant Major Pendry manages to simplify complex concepts and put them into words we all can understand and profit by. His use of examples and diagrams makes it easy to follow. When he adds a few theories of his own, they help to clarify and complement the more difficult concepts. The end result is a splendid and at times humorous book that once started is hard to put down.

Noncommissioned officers are, at this very moment around the world, leading, training, and caring for soldiers. That's what we expect of them and it's been that way for more than 200 years. Most, if not all, of the sage advice from NCOs goes unrecorded, lost to all but a few who pass it on to the next generations of corporals and sergeants. Command Sergeant Major Pendry has corrected this problem by providing *The Three-Meter Zone* for our future guidance. I hope the book inspires other NCOs to record their own leadership lessons, making it the first of many such publications.

The Three-Meter Zone was written by one of the NCO Corps best and brightest noncommissioned officers. He discusses army values in "user friendly" terms. It is well written with important messages for army leaders, past, present, and future.

I highly recommend that all NCOs, both active and reserve component, read *The Three-Meter Zone* and make it a permanent part of their personal professional libraries.

Command Sergeant Major Jimmie Spencer, USA (Ret.)

INTRODUCTION

Noncommissioned officers (NCOs) are great teachers —arguably the best in the world. Still, we don't always do a good job teaching leadership. What we teach and how we teach it cause soldiers to memorize lists of traits, principles, characteristics, and leadership theories. When they can recite these lists, we believe we've taught them leadership. We need to concentrate on how soldiers really learn to lead and follow. We'll do a better job of teaching them if we do.

I believe there are three types of soldiers. I call them three-meter, fifty-meter, and 100-meter soldiers. Each type requires a different level or style of leadership. This book talks about each in detail. I also believe that all levels of leadership are important. The most important and critical leadership, however, takes place between the soldier and the first line noncommissioned leader. This is the leadership that happens at the first level—in the three-meter zone.

Soldiers don't learn to lead or follow from generals. They learn from other soldiers. Reading what is written by and about our nation's greatest generals teaches them about our army, its history, and the generals' careers. Leadership theory written by professionals holding impressive credentials teaches how leadership could or should work in a perfect world. Soldiers learn our basic leadership manual and commit many principles and factors, and all the be, know, and do attributes to memory. At the end of the day, though, all a soldier learns about leading and following is learned from another soldier—a noncommissioned officer.

By example, we teach soldiers how to follow and lead. Both are arts for soldiers to master. A soldier is exposed to many leaders in the army. The most important and influential leader for a soldier is always the closest one: the one in the three-meter zone.

> Every soldier is a leader regardless of his rank or position. His attitude, opinions, desires and deportment mold the approach to mission taken by those above him and his subordinates. It is the summation of this leadership by 'every soldier' that makes our Army a winner. —Department of the Army Pamphlet 600-65, November 1985, *author unknown*

Leaders are not always senior in rank. For me, the most valuable leadership lessons always have come from the example of the leaders closest to me. I still learn from them every day. Some exceptional men and women have taught me valuable lessons over time. Conversely, I have learned from some pitiful ones, too. The soldierly values and work ethic passed to me from those exceptional soldiers taught me to discern between good and bad, right and wrong. They also taught me to examine critically all issues from a soldier's perspective.

I have read books by famous leaders. They are great for personal development and leadership quotes. These great leaders, if they were soldiers, usually attributed some of their success to noncommissioned officers. Most were adamant about that. What I never got from any of these stories was how the noncommissioned officers felt about these relationships and their part in them. What's missing from our leadership teaching of soldiers is the soldiers' and NCOs' perspectives and the realization that we actually teach leadership by our actions.

In *The Three-Meter Zone,* you won't find any lists to memorize, or theories from some doctoral thesis on leadership. There are no career maps or lists of things a leader or NCO is supposed be, know, or do. What you will find is a soldier's perspective on everyday leadership in the three-meter zone.

It's not the intent of this book to provide noncommissioned officers or anyone else a chiseled-in-stone formula for becoming effective leaders. Although many well-credentialed and distinguished scholars of leadership will argue that there is one, I have never been able to find a magic formula for successful leadership. What works for one does not always work for another.

The hope for this book is that it will cause noncommissioned officers to take a critical look at leadership. The purpose of each chapter is to start a discussion and encourage noncommissioned officers to enter their voices into the discussion of leadership. If some of my writing sounds like I'm preaching a sermon, it's because I'm hoping that by offering you a point of view, I'll encourage you to offer yours. That's how we can fill the void in the discussion of leadership. Who better to fill it than the real on-the-ground leaders of our army—noncommissioned officers?

PART ONE: THE LEADER

Leadership is a matter of intelligence, trustworthiness, humaneness, courage, and sternness.
—*Sun Tzu,* The Art of War

If you spend even a short amount of time in the army, sooner or later you will have to perform as a leader. It doesn't matter if you have to lead in combat arms, combat support, or combat service support units. It's important to realize, however, that your opportunity may come on short notice, and it may not be in an environment conducive to your gradual development as a leader. It's never too early to begin your preparation for the eventuality that some day you will lead.

CHAPTER ONE
BUILDING THE FOUNDATION

A foundation is the basis upon which something stands and is supported. A leader, like a structure, must have a solid foundation to stand erect and weather the inevitable storms.

Your Leadership Philosophy

Communications, or the ability to inform people what you expect of them in understandable terms and the ability to transmit to them your interest in them, is the key to successful leadership.
—*Gen. Harold K. Johnson*

Everything we do and are comes from our value systems. How we view and treat others, our work ethic, and our ability to discern right from wrong all stem from our values. We express our values to others by our actions. It's important for us to communicate them orally and in writing, too. Approaching our philosophy like this causes us to do some deep, critical thinking that's probably past due.

The first time I ever thought about the term "leadership philosophy," I figured it was something dreamed up by some old, retired soldier who finally had time to reflect on his greatness. Philosophy, to me, was one of those nerdy college subjects to be avoided. It was the father of some odd discussions. Which came first—the chicken or the egg? Or—If there is no one in the forest to see the tree fall, does it make any noise? I didn't see how any of this applied to being a soldier or leading one.

Curiosity forced me to the dictionary. There I found at least a dozen definitions of philosophy. Reading down the list, I was reaffirming my initial belief that philosophy and leadership were like water and oil. To use a modern buzz-word, the synergy just wasn't there. I was ready to chuck the whole notion until I got to definition number eleven. Old number eleven read, "The system of values by which one lives."

The first battalion commander I had as a command sergeant major sat me down and told me that he wanted to share his leadership philosophy with me and give me a written copy of it. I was instantly leery. I had heard about these guys who gave their command sergeants major letters telling them what their jobs were. I sat back, squinted one eye a little, folded my arms, and listened.

He went over his couple of sheets of paper with me line by line. My scowl began to relax as he started telling me what he was going to do—not what I was going to do. He told me how he liked to be dealt with and how he dealt with others. He laid out his views on training, discipline, quality of life, team building, communication, and many other issues important to leaders. The only thing he said about me was how he viewed our command-team relationship and its importance to the success of the command.

He also laid out for his staff and commanders his expectations of them. He gave a copy of his philosophy to all of his key staff and commanders. He gave us his contract. He gave us his views on important issues and told us how he operated. Then he said, "And you can hold me to it." I punched three holes in that paper and put it in my walking-around notebook. I did hold him to it. He never came up short of what he said he was or what he said he would do.

I figured there had to be something to this idea of writing down a leadership philosophy. So I thought I would try my hand at my own. It made me think about how I felt about communicating, training, counseling, quality of life, and the leadership competencies that are important to leading soldiers. I was surprised at just how little deep, critical thought I had given to what I called my profession—leading soldiers. For things about which I should have had a solid, experience-based opinion, I was drawing a blank.

I was in a real dilemma. I didn't know or couldn't discuss how I felt about important leadership topics. Unit first sergeants and other key noncommissioned officers (NCOs) could not support my position if they didn't know where I was going and how I planned to get there.

Developing, committing to writing, and sharing your philosophy on leading with key people that you rely on is a critical step in taking a leadership role in an organization. As you write down and prepare to share your philosophy, consider some important points. Make sure it's yours. Don't put some words onto a piece of paper because they sound good, and don't make the mistake of writing down how you'd like to be. Write down how you are. It has to be your philosophy. You have to believe it and live it. Because whomever you share it with will hold you to it, just as I did with my commander.

There is no format. List the things important to you as a leader. If you draw a blank, start with the leadership competencies from *Field Manual 22-100, Military Leadership:* communications, supervision, teaching and counseling, soldier-team development, technical and tactical proficiency, decision making, planning, use of available systems, and professional ethics. Think about standards, discipline, training, and physical fitness. When thinking of these and other leadership issues, factor in the values of candor, courage, commitment, competence, and compassion. Forget book answers. Write down your honest feelings and thoughts about each.

Each soldier has his own set of values developed in his home, place of worship, school, and community. But when an individual leaves civilian life and puts on the army uniform he incurs new obligations based on army values. Through strengthening individual values of candor, competence, courage, and commitment [add compassion], these values of the professional army ethic can be developed as the working values of all soldier teams. The role of the leader is not to change long-held personal values, but to impress upon the soldier the importance of these professional values. If, however, a soldier holds values that significantly conflict with these army values, the leader must seek some resolution with the soldier. —Field Manual 22-102, *1987*

Remember. Your philosophy is "the system of values by which [you live]." This time it's your system of values. If what you write is honest and you don't like it, reassess. When you are through, if all you can manage is a list, maybe you ain't ready to lead soldiers.

Values

Values are attitudes about the worth or importance of people, concepts, or things. Values influence your behavior because you use them to decide between alternatives. . . . Your values will influence your priorities. Strong values are what you put first, defend most, and want least to give up.
—Field Manual 22-100, *1990*

Our army is a values-based organization. That's what has made it and will continue to make it a great army. Throughout the years, we have all seen slight changes to those values—the words. What has never changed is our reliance on them as our foundation. Currently, the army embraces seven core values identified by the acronym LDRSHIP. They are loyalty, duty, respect, selfless service, honor, integrity, and personal courage. In the discussion that follows, I'll talk about those, but I'll also talk about other values that have served us well and that, like any strong foundation, have stood the test of time.

We talk a lot about the army's personal values—candor, courage, commitment, competence, and compassion—and the values of the army ethic: loyalty, duty, selfless service, integrity, and the latest additions of honor and personal respect. We say they're the foundation for all we do. Our doctrine calls them the bedrock of our army.

Everyone knows how the leadership manual defines our values. Unfortunately, too many of us stop thinking about them right there. If you don't buy that, then try this. Stop right now and take out your Skilcraft pen and your little green notebook. Write in your notebook what each value means to you personally. Be honest. You may find out that although the words are nice you've never given much serious thought to their meaning as values. You have to do that if you're to embrace them as your values. To claim the army's values as your own, you must be clear on what they mean to you personally and how you apply them to your everyday life.

Courage

Courage is resistance to fear, mastery of fear—not absence of fear. —*Mark Twain*

I never felt very comfortable talking about courage until I gave it some thought. That's probably because our culture has conditioned us to believe it's something unknown. "You'll never know until the time comes," people say. Many believe you're not qualified to speak of courage unless you've faced an enemy in combat. I felt that way myself for many years. But courage as a value is more than that. Remaining in control of your fears and doing what has to be done in the face of danger is a product of the value of courage inculcated through actions in your daily life.

Courage means taking a stand for what is morally and ethically right and not wilting under the fears or threats of losing your status or career. If you succumb to pressures to do other than what you know is right, in my mind at least, you will readily give in to the fears of physical harm and death and be unable to carry out your duties in a hostile, dangerous environment.

It's unfortunate, but many of us make decisions based on their political correctness or popularity instead of on whether they're the right decisions. Most people, in any organization, are well informed enough to realize when a leadership decision is motivated by self-preservation instead of what's right. That's how we too often represent the value of courage. A leader who makes decisions based on self-preservation in one situation will do the same in another. That will not teach the value of courage.

Candor

Say what you have to say. Not what you ought.
—*Henry David Thoreau*

Mr. Thoreau pretty much defined candor when he said that. Every time we open our mouths, someone, somewhere, will not agree with or will be offended by what we say. It's just a part of our world today. Because of that, some of us spend too much time constructing statements so they are politically correct and easy on everyone's ears. When we do that, we end up with watered-down, ambiguous, but politically correct speech—not what we know needs to be said.

That's not how you teach candor. Our own accepted definition of candor is being frank, open, honest, and sincere with subordinates, seniors, and peers. That means saying what has to be said, and sometimes saying it without smoothing the rough edges off it.

Another problem with candor is the shotgun-blast approach often used to tell people they're messing up. A shotgun blast starts out like this: "We have a problem because some of you are not . . ." That approach lets everyone hear about a problem of which they may not be guilty, while the guilty may not know the shotgun is actually aimed at them. You teach candor by confronting the guilty party directly and privately, and saying, "Smith, we have a problem because you are not . . ."

Some leaders insist that candor is being able to look subordinates in the eye and tell them they're not measuring up. Good leaders do that, but that's not candor. That's a leadership expectation. Candor is when you look your best friend and peer in the eye and say, "You ain't measuring up." When candor is a value, best friends accept honest criticism from a peer and a friend, and act on it. You must encourage this kind of exchange and be willing to accept this openness and honesty from subordinates as well. You teach candor by practicing it.

Competence

Competence is my watchword. —*The NCO Creed*

What is competence as a value? It's a lot more than just doing your job to an acceptable standard. If you claim competence as a value, you take frequent inventory of your skills, knowledge, and attitudes. Then you take action to improve in areas that need it and to acquire the skills, knowledge, and attitudes you don't have. When competence is a value, this process is continuous.

Leaders holding competence as a value constantly look to improve themselves and their organizations. Leaders who work at their competence have confidence in their abilities. Their self-confidence makes others more confident in them and in their units' ability to get the job done. When soldiers see you continually working at self-improvement, they accept competence as a value and follow your example.

Commitment

[Being in the army means a] total commitment to a higher calling, devotion to duty and a thousand other adjectives. —*Sgt. Maj. of the Army Glen E. Morrell*

Commitment is a big word, but it gets only a small mention in our leadership manual. A commitment is a pledge or obligation to do something. If you say you're committed to something, you obligate yourself to do it. When you insist you are a part of a group—the army—you pledge to uphold the values, traditions, and standards of that group.

The first thing you must commit to is accepting and living by the army values we've been talking about. You have to commit to your job and the responsibilities you incur as a leader. Being committed to a job means being committed to the job you have now—not the one you hope to have later. Commitment to a job now will always ensure your future. Your most important commitment must be to people—your soldiers, peers, leaders, and family.

The army is a culture and a way of life that's different from any other. You must commit to accepting that way of life and becoming a full part of it. If you want to be a successful member of a successful organization, you have to commit to it. Life is different inside the gate than it is outside. You can travel back and forth between them, but you must accept and exist in one or the other. You must commit.

Compassion

Compassion is the deep feeling of sharing the suffering of another, together with the inclination to give aid or support, or to show mercy. It's a complex, confusing, and sometimes contradictory value for soldiers. The difficult question for soldiers is: How can I give aid or support or show mercy to an enemy that it's my mission to destroy?

I cannot imagine that any worthwhile leader of soldiers would risk unnecessary casualties. That's compassion shown toward the leader's own soldiers. The leader shows the same compassion when ensuring that unnecessary casualties are not inflicted on an already defeated enemy. When compassion is a value, that's what happens, and that's what an army that holds compassion as a value does.

Compassion means understanding and sharing difficult times with people and their families. When they hurt, you feel it, and when they feel joy, so do you. It means treating everyone with the dignity and respect they deserve. Sometimes it means listening to and understanding your emotions instead of trying to control them.

Respect

Officers of my unit will have maximum time to accomplish their duties; they will not have to accomplish mine. I will earn their respect and confidence as well as that of my soldiers. —*The NCO Creed*

The key word in the quote from the NCO creed is not *respect*. It's *earn*. Our position and rank, the medals we wear, and many other things you can think of are said to command respect. Sure, they'll get you all the formal trappings of respect, because the code we abide by in the military requires it. But respect for those things is much different from respect for people. When we talk of respect as a value, we are talking about people. I'm sure you've heard the expression "I respect his position" or similar expressions. That's much different from saying, "I respect him."

To earn respect, you have to show respect. Like all values, respect starts with us. We must first demonstrate that we respect ourselves. Simply put, that means selecting and living a healthy lifestyle and doing those things necessary to make us better soldiers and leaders. When you respect yourself, showing respect for others is easy. Demonstrating a willingness to show consideration for or appreciation of others will earn you the same treatment. After that, work at taking care of soldiers and your own professional competence, and you'll earn respect.

Loyalty

I will be loyal to those with whom I serve, seniors, peers and subordinates alike. —*The NCO Creed*

When you read about loyalty in *Field Manual 22-100* or hear it discussed, a lot of high ideals are expressed: loyalty to the nation, the Constitution, Old Glory, the American way of life, and apple pie. Those are great thoughts we all understand. Loyalty as a value for soldiers starts at a much more basic level than that.

Loyalty starts with soldiers being loyal to one another. Without loyalty to our teammates, other high ideals are not achievable. Or, as one of the charter members of my personal three-meter zone expresses it, "It's like breathing a lot of rarified air." In other words, high ideals make you feel a little giddy, but when you get back down to earth, you find that nothing's changed.

I was privileged to listen to a Medal of Honor recipient discussing the importance of loyalty to one another. I doubt I can convey the emotion he expressed when discussing this thought. Nor can I tell you what his thoughts were when he got a distant look in his eyes, but the words he said were spoken with deep feeling and conviction. He convinced me about where loyalty starts.

Relying on his personal experience, he said that when soldiers find themselves in dangerous, life-threatening situations, they don't fight for high ideals. They fight for their teammates, and everything they do is because they care deeply for one another. They are intensely loyal and willing to sacrifice for each other. The value of loyalty starts with teammates who care for and are loyal to each other.

Duty

> In our army every soldier must care about his job. Often, if the duty seems menial or humdrum, it is hard to cultivate this attitude. But it must be done. . . . What you do in your job each day, you do for the army. —*Sgt. Maj. of the Army William O. Wooldridge*

Duty is a value built on a solid foundation of self-discipline. If duty is one of your values, you can be counted on to do what must be done without being reminded to do it. You do the boring things with the same zeal with which you do the exciting and challenging things. You use the same preciseness and thoroughness performing harmless tasks as you use performing dangerous ones. You understand your obligations to your soldiers, your unit, and the army, and you fulfill them with a sense of urgency.

Holding duty as a value means you are willing to do what must be done and are ready to accept the responsibility for and the consequences of doing what's right and necessary. It means you'll tell the truth as you see it to your soldiers and your superiors. You'll do that even if the truth is not pleasant, and even if it doesn't offer the best picture of you or your unit.

Selfless Service

> I will not use my grade or position to attain pleasure, profit, or personal safety. —*The NCO Creed*

Anyone who reads what I write can tell you that my English grammar skills need work. But I do remember some basic rules. When the suffix "-less" is added to the word *self,* for example, it means that the self is no longer a factor. Selfless service, then, means that the self is not a factor in the performance of your duties or service.

As a value, it means that you do not base your actions on what you might stand to lose or gain personally. Service to your soldiers and your unit always has priority over your personal desires. It means you live up to our creed and never use your rank or position for personal gain or safety. Selfless service is an important value. When it's demonstrated by leaders, it builds cohesion, teamwork, and units filled with soldiers committed to service to their units.

Honor

> I would lay down my life for America, but I cannot trifle with my honor. —*John Paul Jones*

Honor is a code we live by. It encompasses all our values and all that we do. When honor is a value, it means we will do what we say and live by the values we express as ours. It means we live by a code of dignity, integrity, and pride. It also means that our personal integrity is maintained without any legal or other obligation. A code of honor is an uncompromising commitment to a way of life.

Integrity

An honest man's the noblest work of God.
—*Alexander Pope*

Every structure requires a solid foundation. The values we each hold are the foundation of our army. The cornerstone for all the values we've discussed is integrity. Without a foundation built on integrity, the entire value system collapses. You first have to be honest with yourself, because that's where integrity as a value begins. If you can't be honest with your own self-assessments, there is no chance you will be honest with others. Integrity is the foundation for the trust and confidence that your soldiers must have in you if there is any chance for you to be a successful leader.

Without integrity there is no value system. Without a value system there is no foundation for our army. No institution can stand without a solid foundation. It's that simple.

Trust and Confidence

Candor is honesty and faithfulness to the truth. . . . Team members must be able to trust one another and their leaders. Without truthfulness this will not occur. —Field Manual 22-102, *March 1987*

"For reasons I'm not at liberty to discuss." That's how, during a telephone conversation, a charter member of my personal three-meter zone told me a trusted leader broke a commitment to him—a commitment made face to face and sealed with a handshake.

He told me that the reason he didn't get the job he was promised was never explained to him. Sometimes leaders have to break commitments to soldiers. When we do, our values require us to be forthright and candid enough to explain why. Without an explanation, soldiers draw their own conclusions about why commitments—promises— are broken. Those conclusions are drawn based on what the soldiers know, perceive, or have been told by someone else. Conclusions drawn by soldiers and based on partial or no information lead to a loss of trust and confidence in the leader—trust and confidence the leader may never regain.

> Trust, like the soul, never returns once it is gone.
> —*Publilius Syrus*

A soldier will also question a leader's sincerity and motivations in the future based on those previously drawn conclusions. Worse yet, the soldier may share his or her story with other soldiers, as my friend did, resulting in an even larger loss of trust.

Let me tell you the side of the story I know, and maybe it will help to illustrate the point. I can only tell you my friend's side, because the other side (for reasons his leader "was not at liberty to discuss") was never shared with him. Draw your own conclusions as he did, and as any soldier might.

While deactivating a battalion in Germany, my friend had a discussion with his leader about a future assignment.

His superior told him he was recommended for an assignment that would open at the same time as his battalion deactivated. The leader asked him if he wanted the job, and my friend said yes. He then told my friend, while looking him in the eye and shaking his hand, "I'm going to make that happen." The leader was in a position to deliver on his promise. My friend told me, "When we shook hands and I walked out of his office, I never doubted it would happen."

About one month before he was supposed to report to his new job, my friend received assignment instructions sending him elsewhere. Having total confidence in his leader's commitment, he told the assignment folks there was a mistake. They assured him, after discussing it with his leader, that his new assignment instructions were accurate.

After a week of trying, he was finally able to talk to his leader about the change made to his assignment. The leader declined to see him in person; instead, he talked to him on the phone. He never discussed the reason for the change with my friend, but gave him the one-line explanation noted previously, and wished him luck.

You may be thinking that this kind of thing happens all the time in the army. And you're right; it does. The difference is that those affected usually know why. The other part of the story is that the person who got the job promised to my friend was a known personal friend of this leader. Maybe there was a logical and reasonable explanation for what happened. If there was, the leader made a critical mistake by never sharing that explanation with my friend.

When such changes are not explained to soldiers, they draw their own conclusions, right or wrong, based on what they know or perceive. My friend's conclusions caused him to lose trust in the leader and question his motivations—then and now. The bigger problem is that other soldiers with whom my friend shared this story, including me, also lost trust in this leader.

I think about this story often and recall the dejected look on my friend's face as he was telling it to me. The story caused me to do some serious soul searching about trust. It made me wonder if I had done something similar to a subordinate or a friend. What's sad is that I probably have. Most importantly, it made me think about trust and confidence and the potential I have to lose both every time I make a commitment to a soldier or to anyone. I lost trust in this leader, but his actions taught me a valuable leadership lesson about how fragile trust is and how easily it can be lost.

> Trust is the cornerstone of loyalty. If our subordinates, comrades, and superiors trust us, loyalty follows easily. —*Gen. John A. Wickham, Jr.*

This leader always stressed the importance of communication and keeping soldiers informed. A short explanation, even if over the phone, may have helped him keep my friend's trust and confidence and, as an extension, mine and that of others. The lack of an explanation ensured the opposite.

Toolbox Inventory

> Competence is my watchword. . . . I will strive to stay tactically and technically proficient. —*The NCO Creed*

Are those familiar words? After getting in touch with and communicating our own value system—our philosophy—there is another critical block to add to the leadership foundation. That is finding out if we have the necessary tools to carry out our philosophy.

The first thing to do in operating as a leader is be honest with yourself. The problem is, there is much rhetoric in this business. There is not enough honesty with ourselves about just who we are and whether we are really perceived as [leaders] by our subordinates. An honest-to-God, soul-searching self-evaluation is in order—and very difficult to do. I think this is the first vital step as one goes about the business of becoming a better leader.
—*Gen. William Livsey*

I watched a training video in which a general talks about leadership and the important role sergeants play in developing soldiers and leaders. In the video, the general attributes much of his success to a sergeant. The sergeant, his first platoon sergeant as a lieutenant, took him to the motor pool and told him his first task was to inventory his toolbox.

By the time he completed the toolbox inventory, he had touched and examined the condition of all of his tools. He knew right away which tools were missing. Of what was there, he knew which ones needed to be replaced or repaired. He immediately set about replacing missing and unserviceable tools. After all, the platoon could not do its maintenance work without the right tools.

Being a successful noncommissioned officer, like any job, requires the right tools. Just as it did for the general, success for NCOs starts with a toolbox inventory. The inventory is an honest self-assessment of attitudes, knowledge, and skills. It tells us our strengths and weaknesses. Just as it did for the general, it tells us what tools we have and their condition.

An accurate, thorough inventory is the foundation for success; we are not ready to be effective noncommissioned officers until we complete one. Completing the inventory, our honest self-assessment, is not easy. It's human to rationalize away weaknesses instead of accepting and dealing with them.

"I smoke because I like it. It relaxes me. It makes me feel good."

"I have big bones."

It is easier to accept rationalizations like these than to admit that we might not be tough enough to kick a life-threatening habit or that we might be too heavy. The downside is that rationalizations take away our ability to make honest self-assessments. The result is a personal toolbox inventory that is not accurate. It doesn't tell us which tools we have and what condition they are in.

The drawback to a rationalized inventory is concentrating on the tools we have that work well so much that we never get around to fixing what's broken.

When NCOs turn in rationalized inventories, it adversely affects the soldiers they lead and their units. Soldiers get really good at what their NCOs do well, and not so good at what they don't do well. If an NCO is a distinguished marksman, for example, that NCO's unit is probably a cut above average in marksmanship. If a first sergeant is a stickler for following the training management doctrine in *Field Manual 25-101, Battle Focused Training,* you can count on the other NCOs in the unit also being well versed.

Overemphasis on the things we do well impacts the whole unit. We all know units that are very good at one or two things. A unit's strong suit may be physical training, for example. Sometimes that's a result of leadership focusing on what it likes and is good at to the detriment of other programs. When that happens, it's because the unit's leadership never turned in an accurate toolbox inventory. Or, if they did, they took no action to replace and/or repair missing and broken tools.

Unit leaders' concentrating on what they do well is duplicated in every part of a unit, including the individual soldier. The motor pool has the best transmission mechanic. The personnel administration center has the best awards clerk. Soldiers, following the example of their leaders, learn to concentrate on what they do very well to the detriment of other necessary skills. The unit leadership successfully transfers a "do one thing real good" mentality to the whole unit.

Another drawback to inaccurate toolbox inventories is that we end up with small comfort zones in which to operate. What we are not good at makes us uncomfortable when we are confronted with it. It takes us out of our comfort zones. It's human nature to avoid being uncomfortable; so, because of discomfort, we fail to work at getting better.

The challenge is to use accurate inventories to work at

improving weaknesses until they are brought into our comfort zones. Our comfort zones define the size of our toolboxes. NCOs have to view every educational opportunity and experience as a chance to add tools to the box, and thus improve the skills with which we are not comfortable. The larger we make our comfort zones—our toolboxes—the more tools we can put into them. The more tools that are available to us, the more effective we and our soldiers are.

I recall listening to Gen. Colin Powell in a press briefing during the Gulf War. He was asked about the possibility of using nuclear weapons against the Iraqi army. The general said something like, "When I go to do a job, I bring my toolbox. In the toolbox is a whole selection of tools that I might need. When I have all my tools with me, then I am able to select the appropriate one for the job."

To inventory our toolboxes, we need a list of the tools that should be present—a list found in a couple of places. There is no technical manual to tell us their working condition. That determination comes from an honest-to-God, soul-searching self-evaluation.

A good starting point for your inventory list is Chapter 3 of *Training Circular 22-6, The Noncommissioned Officer's Guide.* Inventory the list of attitudes the NCO guide describes as the attitudes all noncommissioned officers must possess. These are our basic tools, which are the first things we should find in the toolbox. The assessment is simple. When you inventory your attitudes, ask the questions "Do I?" and "Am I?" Asking questions is easy. Giving yourself a self-assessing honest answer is the hard part.

Do I enforce standards, set the example, accomplish the mission, take care of soldiers, accept responsibility for self and subordinates, obey lawful orders, maintain physical and mental toughness, show competence and self-confidence, act fairly and equitably with subordinates, and show initiative and self-motivation?

Am I dedicated and selfless, honest and courageous, loyal to the nation and the Constitution, and loyal to superiors, peers, and subordinates?

What is the condition of the attitudes in your toolbox? Are they all accounted for and in working order? Honestly?

Continue your inventory using the lists of skills and knowledge from the NCO guide for your rank. The primary tools for skills and knowledge are also the leadership competencies found in *Field Manual 22-100, Military Leadership:* communication, supervision, teaching and counseling, soldier-team development, technical and tactical proficiency, decision making, planning, use of available systems, and professional ethics. Under each primary tool is the list of parts required to make it an operational system.

For skills, look at the parts and answer honestly the questions "Can I?" and "Do I?" For example, "Can I or do I issue clear and concise orders to small groups?" For knowledge, examine the parts list and ask, "Do I know?" For example, under communication: "Do I know listening and watching principles?" Or, under supervision: "Do I know the unit's standing operating procedures?" Carefully examine each of the components that make up an NCO's basic toolbox. After you have determined what's there and the condition it's in, you'll know what you need to do.

Once you are satisfied that all of your tools are in the box and in working condition, you can assess your ability to use them. You do that with Part IV of the *Noncommissioned Officer Evaluation Report,* "Values and NCO Responsibilities."

Your tools are what you need to do the basic job. The *Noncommissioned Officer Evaluation Report* is the system that measures how well you use your tools. It is very difficult to step back and take a look at yourself. Remember our tendency to rationalize? Take a step toward being a successful NCO by completing your toolbox inventory. Do it honestly, and you'll find it educational and worthwhile.

Attitudes

Units live and die by the attitudes of soldiers and leaders. So do individuals. An attitude is a position. It's the posture you take when dealing with a subject. You cannot instill an attitude in soldiers; instead, you show them by example what a proper one is. You have to convince them that a positive attitude supporting the legal and moral position of the unit is critical to the unit's success.

Think of any topic at all, no matter how obscure it might be. You have an attitude about it—a position. So does every soldier in your unit. What's critical for the army is for soldiers to support the common position or attitude of the organization. Attitudes, like every other form of behavior, are learned. Soldiers learn their attitudes or positions from noncommissioned officers— their role models.

Noncommissioned officers must project positive and supportive attitudes. If a decision is made, and it is legal and moral, put your personal feelings aside and support it. How many times have you met this guy? "This ain't my idea, it's old so-and-so's." Or, "This will never work." Too many times, I expect. These attitudes and positions violate two basic rules and guarantee failure.

The first statement is what you hear from a weak noncommissioned officer unwilling to support an unpopular but necessary decision. He is more concerned with popularity than with doing the right thing. This sends a message to soldiers: "We have to do the mission, but we don't have to put much heart into it." That attitude reflects on both soldier and unit performance, resulting in a job that is just good enough to get by—a D-minus grade.

Soldiers will support you and whatever attitude you take. They are in constant contact with you and think it's acceptable to discount old so-and-so, especially when you do it. Noncommissioned officers are obligated to adopt and support leadership decisions as their own. A decision has to come across to soldiers as "ours," never "his," "hers," or "theirs."

The second statement, "It'll never work," ensures failure. Noncommissioned officers make things work or fail based largely on the positive or negative attitudes they display. In Germany a few years ago, I watched a program called Single Soldier Initiatives enjoy great success in some units while being a dismal failure in others. The reason for failure or success in each unit was directly tied to NCO attitudes. The noncommissioned officers in units in which the program failed said, "It'll never work." Every action they took was to prove the program would fail, rather than to make it work.

Decisions that are fully supported usually will work, but the greatest plan ever made is doomed to failure if it is not supported. NCOs are operators and mission executors, making things succeed or fail in the army. It all relates to the difference between positive and negative attitudes. Soldiers learn their attitudes from noncommissioned officers. Do you want to ensure failure or success? The answer to that question determines the attitude you project to soldiers. You may not claim ownership of a decision, but you will not be able to disown the failure that comes from a negative attitude.

When it comes to being successful as a leader, nothing can replace the effect of a positive attitude projected to soldiers.

Check Your System

The aim of leadership is not merely to find and record failures in men, but to remove the causes of failure. —*Dr. W. Edwards Deming*

The good doctor got to the heart of leadership with those words. Dr. Deming is credited with being the father of the total-quality philosophy of management. It's the approach that rebuilt Japan into an economic powerhouse and producer of quality products after World War II. Now, I know old soldiers cringe whenever you try to mix the words *management* and *leadership* in the same conversation. "You manage things; you lead people" is the common expression, and I totally agree.

The fundamental ideas of treating people with dignity and respect and of continuous improvement, which are expressed in our leadership and training doctrines, plainly embrace Dr. Deming's philosophy. With that as a starting point, let's talk about the good doctor's prescription for successful leadership measured in terms of quality.

Deming stresses systems and their supporting processes as the keys to quality products. In his book, *The New Economics*, he states that the aim of management in the system is to "achieve the best results for everybody—everybody [wins]."

From my point of view, the aim of leadership is the same. For this discussion, let's call the army our system and leadership its most important process. The product of the army's leadership process is quality soldiers that admirably represent our nation and are able to fight, win, and survive on the modern battlefield.

When a product fails, according to Deming, we are likely to find the reason for the failure by evaluating the process used to make it. Therefore, he reasons, an evaluation of the process must come before an evaluation of the people using it. That is a sound and basic approach to leadership.

Following this logic, if a trained and fully qualified soldier (our raw material) enters our leadership process and fails, the failure is traceable to a flaw in the process. Simply put, the process produces the failure. Just as quality products come from the best processes, quality soldiers come from the best leadership processes.

Whenever a soldier fails, our usual first step is an evaluation of the soldier—the product of our leadership process. It's not unusual to examine a substandard or broken product, but what also needs to happen is a hard look at the leadership process that produced a soldier unable to meet a standard—a broken product.

Deming tells us to capture a process on a flowchart and use it to find the flawed steps. Then we can fix them. If our product is a soldier, we ought to be able to flowchart the leadership process that produced the soldier.

To illustrate the point, I have charted two versions of the leadership process. The first chart is the Einstein Insanity Version (Figure 1). I call it that because it proves Einstein's definition of insanity, which is doing the same thing over and over while hoping for a different result.

The input to the leadership process is one fully qualified soldier—the product of our initial entry training system. Our desired output or product is a fully qualified soldier who can fight, win, and survive, and a process that enables the soldier to maintain qualifications. The Army Physical Fitness Test is the leadership challenge used to test the process. Any leadership challenge will work, however. The first version of the process works well as long as everyone passes the test. Unfortunately, it's the one too often found in army units—the Einstein Insanity Version.

When a soldier fails a test, we evaluate the soldier, put that soldier in special fitness training, and bring him or her back up to standards. After this, we give the soldier (the product of this process) back to the process that produced a failure (a broken product) in the first place—insanity defined.

When the insanity process fails the second time, we compound the problem. We separate the soldier (our product), in whom we have invested time and resources, from the army. We throw our broken product away. Then,

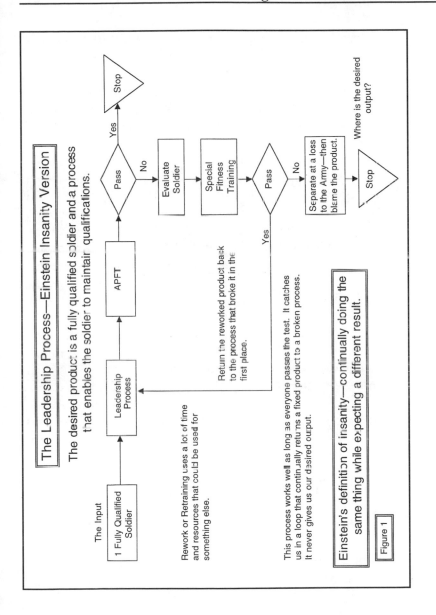

The Leadership Process—Einstein Insanity Version

The desired product is a fully qualified soldier and a process that enables the soldier to maintain qualifications.

The Input

1 Fully Qualified Soldier

Leadership Process

APFT

Pass — Yes → Stop

Pass — No → Evaluate Soldier → Special Fitness Training → Pass

Rework or Retraining uses a lot of time and resources that could be used for something else.

Return the reworked product back to the process that broke it in the first place.

Pass — No → Separate at a loss to the Army—then blame the product. → Stop

Where is the desired output?

This process works well as long as everyone passes the test. It catches us in a loop that continually returns a fixed product to a broken process. It never gives us our desired output.

Einstein's definition of insanity—continually doing the same thing while expecting a different result.

Figure 1

31

instead of examining the process, we tend to blame the failure on the product. Can you imagine a business surviving that way? The army cannot survive that way either, considering today's personnel and resource cuts. The Insanity Version gives us individually repaired or reworked products, but never gives us our desired output—a fixed product and a process that keeps it fixed.

Following the doctor's prescription, we can analyze the process with our flowchart and fix it. I wrestled with that thought for a while. Remember that Deming is adamant that we spend time evaluating processes, not people. However, in the army, we must evaluate people. How could I address that and still follow the doctor's advice? As I thought about it, it became clear.

In the leadership process, we are technically not evaluating people. We are evaluating our product, a fully qualified soldier, to ensure that it meets acceptable standards of quality. Like any business, we first have to ensure that our product is of a high enough quality to do what we say it must do. Secondly, we must have an acceptable return on the investment made to produce the product. Some may view this as a dehumanizing approach, but it isn't. If we have the best possible process in place to make and keep soldiers qualified, it improves their survivability and, by extension, the survivability of the army and our nation. If anything, that adds to the human aspect of our business.

The remaining question is: How can this flowcharting business improve our leadership process? We keep returning to the fact that soldiers, our product, must be continually evaluated against measurable standards. But remember, an evaluation of the soldier alone only tells us what's wrong with one soldier. We then take steps to fix that one soldier or product. That's where the breakdown is in the insanity process. We fix one product at a time and always return it to the process that broke it in the first place.

The Total-Quality Version of the leadership process (Figure 2) still evaluates our product—the soldier. What it adds, however, is a parallel evaluation of the leadership process.

Evaluating the process tells us if and how it contributed to the soldier's or product's failure. Using the fitness test example, you may find that the soldier did not participate in a fitness program or that such a program didn't even exist. Both are failures of the leadership process. This enables us to achieve our ultimate output or product—a soldier who meets the standards and a fixed leadership process enabling the soldier to continue to meet the standard. When we do this, using Deming's expression, everybody wins—the army, the soldier, and our customer, the American taxpayer.

Now, is that management or leadership? Whatever your answer, I think you'll agree that before you put leadership into motion, you have to thoroughly check your system. We owe it to our soldiers and to the army to make sure that the leadership process does not produce human or organizational failures. Make sure your foundation includes a sound leadership process.

Summary

• A leader, like a structure, requires a solid foundation in order to stand erect and weather the inevitable storms.

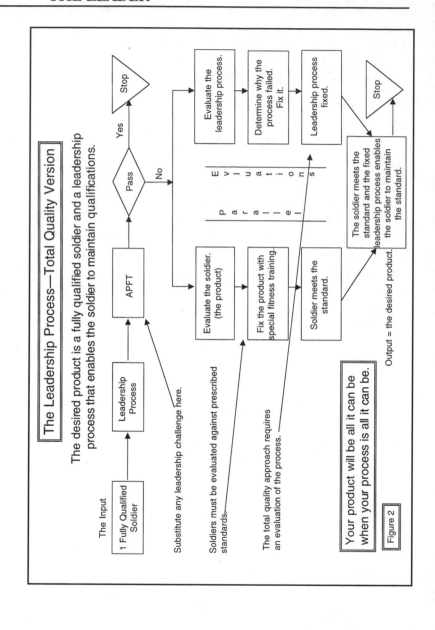

The Leadership Process—Total Quality Version

The desired product is a fully qualified soldier and a leadership process that enables the soldier to maintain qualifications.

The Input

1 Fully Qualified Soldier

Leadership Process

APFT

Pass — Yes — Stop

No

Evaluate the leadership process.

Determine why the process failed. Fix it.

Leadership process fixed.

Stop

Substitute any leadership challenge here.

Soldiers must be evaluated against prescribed standards.

The total quality approach requires an evaluation of the process.

Evaluate the soldier. (the product)

Fix the product with special fitness training.

Soldier meets the standard.

Evaluation Paralleled

The soldier meets the standard and the fixed leadership process enables the soldier to maintain the standard.

Output = the desired product.

Your product will be all it can be when your process is all it can be.

Figure 2

- At the base of the leader's foundation is a philosophy or approach to leading that is held up by a strong set of enduring values, tied together by a code of honor and integrity.
- A strong leader constantly reinforces this foundation by working hard at keeping the trust and confidence of subordinates, peers, and superiors.
- The next layer in the leader's foundation is a process of honest self-assessments that identify weaknesses in his or her knowledge, skills, and abilities, which the leader continuously works to overcome.
- The leader then adds a positive approach to mission accomplishment and taking care of soldiers.
- The last block in the leader's foundation consists of an effective leadership system that accomplishes the mission and produces quality soldiers.

CHAPTER TWO
ESTABLISHING DIRECTION

Leaders must always know what they are about and where they are going. After you establish a solid foundation, based on values and competence, you must establish direction. You have to know where you are going, and you have to know when you get there.

Personal Battle Focus

Sometimes I lie awake at night and ask myself, why am I here? Then a little voice answers, why? Where do you want to be? —*"Peanuts," Charles Schultz*

For units to be effective, they need purpose and direction. They require solid mission statements and solid plans to make sure their missions are accomplished. Otherwise, a unit becomes an organization on a trip with an unknown destination and no roadmaps—it has no direction or purpose. Noncommissioned officers (NCOs), to be effective leaders, must also establish direction and purpose.

An effective NCO works hard at answering Charlie Brown's questions. "Where am I now? Why am I here? Where do I want to be?" Then the NCO adds, "How do I get there?" The NCO deals with those questions using personal battle focus.

Our training system in the army is very effective, with many interlocking steps that produce effective and successful units. First is the commander's training goal, which actually translates into a vision statement—the unit's direction. Then there's the mission statement—the unit's purpose. To work toward the vision and accomplish the mission, a list of mission-essential tasks is developed. Accomplishing those essential tasks requires identifying the training that is needed, from collective to individual. From there we develop plans to accomplish the training and a method of continually assessing where we are and comparing that to where we want to be.

Can you imagine the potential of noncommissioned officers who apply battle-focused principles to their personal lives? Personal battle focus links your leadership philosophy to what you found when you completed your toolbox inventory. In developing your philosophy, you internalized your feelings about important leadership issues; in your toolbox inventory, you identified your strengths and weaknesses. Personal battle focus gives you a plan to project your philosophy, capitalize on your strengths, and vigorously attack your weaknesses. It gives you purpose and direction.

Achieving personal battle focus requires development of a personal vision statement. It's a far-reaching statement describing how you want history to remember you. A personal vision provides you with lifelong direction. After this, develop your personal mission statement by answering a simple question: "What must I do to reach my vision?" Your personal vision and mission are exactly as stated—they're personal. Neither one needs to be complicated, long, or filled with a lot of "can do" mottoes and buzz phrases. What they absolutely must be is yours. Developing effective ones may take a long time.

While developing your personal mission, consider what Dr. Steven Covey calls co-missioning. If you want to be an effective noncommissioned officer, your personal mission must interconnect with and support the army's and your unit's missions.

To reach your personal vision and accomplish your personal mission, you must identify your personal mission-essential tasks. Then, just as you do with your soldiers and your unit, assess your ability to accomplish those tasks. Using battle-focused principles, develop near- and long-term plans to accomplish those essential tasks. Execute your plans. Then continually assess where you are compared to where you want to be.

Personal battle focus, in a nutshell, is applying those principles to ourselves that we apply to units to make them effective. With strong personal vision and mission statements linked to those of your unit and the army, identified essential tasks, a plan to accomplish those tasks, and a method of assessing where you are, you'll be effective. You'll achieve personal battle focus and take an important step in establishing your direction as a leader.

A Good Leader Is . . .

You've probably read plenty about leadership. I have. I have also given up on remembering which expert wrote which book or espoused which theory. There are a lot of leaders, or want-to-be leaders, who can and will tell you about all the theories and approaches to leadership. They even tell you, with conviction, the best approaches to take—usually the methods they are most familiar with. They all know what a good leader is. Or do they?

I told you in the beginning that soldiers don't learn to lead by reading someone's theory on leadership. They learn from watching leaders—usually the ones closest to them. Established leaders can also become better by listening to and learning from soldiers. Soldiers talk about leaders—good ones and bad ones. Soldiers believing a leader is good or not is what it's really all about. Simply put, soldiers will show you what it takes to be a good leader if you listen to them; you just have to pay attention and decide if you want to be one or not.

I attended some training once with a mixed group of military and army civilians. A facilitator put us into workgroups. Each group was assigned to make a list of attributes of their best boss or leader. This was an enlightening exercise. It involved real people listing the attributes that they believed made a good leader. I thought the information was important enough to write down. After comparing the four lists and eliminating some duplication, I came up with one. With four groups working independently, it's amazing how similar the lists were.

According to the composite list I constructed, a good leader:

- Cares for people
- Is trusting

- Is competent and knowledgeable about his or her work
- Empowers subordinates to do their jobs and accepts honest mistakes
- Is honest, ethical, and open
- Is supportive and has a positive attitude
- Is courageous, makes decisions and accepts the consequences, does not lead by fear, and has the courage to say no
- Has a vision for the organization
- Is approachable and a good listener
- Is flexible
- Is sincere
- Gives clear guidance, is a communicator and teacher, has a clear and consistent leadership philosophy, and has realistic expectations
- Is mission-focused—a team player who provides time and resources to get the job done
- Has a sense of humor
- Uses common sense, thinks before acting, and makes intelligent and reasonable decisions
- Passes credit to subordinates

I compared this list to the material in the army's leadership manual, *Field Manual 22-100*. All the attributes turned up there in one form or another in the leadership competencies, traits, and principles, and in the "be, know, and do" attributes. When I compared them, I also discovered that they all fit very neatly onto another foundation: the one built on courage, candor, competence, commitment, and compassion.

The Three Ps Problem

After being a first sergeant for about a year, I read an article in *Parameters Magazine* titled "The Army's Command Sergeant Major Problem," by John C. Bahnsen and James W. Bradin (June 1988). My first take on this article was that a couple of retired senior officers (Retired Brigadier General Bahnsen and Retired Colonel Bradin) were using command sergeants major to vent their frustrations about what were actually command problems, not command sergeant major problems. I was outraged that two officers would attack something that I thought every noncommissioned officer in the army aspired to be.

The Command Sergeant Major Program, an institution representing all that was right with a profession, was being attacked and summarily executed by two senior officers. It was portrayed as an out-of-focus program driven by "the three Ps": perks, privileges, and politics. How could this be? They were wrong, and I was outraged that they would say such things—and in a forum seen mostly by officers. How could they attack my corps? What had made them so bitter? Their conclusions were totally wrong!

Or were they?

Yeah, they were wrong on most things they said. To them, it was a bad thing if a command sergeant major was physically fit; they pointed out in a negative vein that "many of the better-known CSMs are long-distance runners." Conversely, being overweight and undereducated were alluded to as good things, though not accepted in today's army. I also assumed while reading this article that

41

to these distinguished senior officers, a good command sergeant major would be a falling-down drunk. "Rumor has it that in some circles, CSMs don't drink more than two beers except in their own backyards."

They made many similar comments, which really led me to question whether they were discussing the same army I knew. For instance, they implied that the occasional beating of a soldier was unfortunate, but acceptable. "[Henry] was a master carpenter, exceptionally strong physically, and could whip any soldier in the battalion—something, unfortunately, he would do occasionally when a soldier got out of line." Correcting a soldier's behavior through counseling, corrective training, or the Uniform Code of Military Justice (UCMJ), if necessary, apparently was not as acceptable to these officers as using old Hank's technique of just whipping his ass. I thought that was great advice to be coming from senior officers and to be published in one of our service's professional journals.

To say the least, I was infuriated after I finished this article (a big word for really pissed, in case you're reading this, Frank, Henry, or Don—I only mention that because of the great lengths these officers went to in mentioning your collective lack of formal education). The directional arrows on my leadership compass were going a little wacky.

I made a copy anyway. It became, for me, something to pull out and read whenever I had the need to hate somebody. I have kept that copy and carried it around with me since. I've read it through dozens of times, each time making notes on it—so many notes, in fact, that it's becoming difficult to read the article. My notes have become a counterattack on every negative thing the article had to say about our "exalted CSM" program.

I had some frightful things to say about these officers, but using old Frank's "we're not worthy" technique— "[Frank] never initiated comments about officers, except in praise"—I'll just keep them to myself for now. I even had some less-than-complimentary things to say about the comments attributed to Frank, Henry, and Don.

Frank, Henry, and Don were the three sergeants major used by these officers as examples of what sergeants major should be. Their treatment by the senior officers made them come across more like Curly, Larry, and Moe. By the time I got to the closing sentences in this article, I was certain that no court in the land would convict a "rarified and perfumed prince, fitter to carry a tale than a rifle or a wounded comrade" for punching one, or both, of these jokers (and Curly, Larry, and Moe) right in the kisser.

I believed that over the years, I would mellow out some and not get madder than hell every time I read this article. Well, I haven't mellowed much. I still believe that 98 percent of it is the purest form of bovine scatology I've ever read. I think it also represents whining by two insecure senior officers who didn't have the courage to make their feelings known to their general before they retired. That 2 percent they brought out clearly, however, is causing some problems for our NCO corps, and we have to deal with it.

That 2 percent comes like three straight, hard, stinging jabs hitting us square on the mouth. They cut and hurt. It doesn't matter how much we bob and weave and dance around. Every time that 2 percent comes into play, our "exalted CSM" corps and our NCO corps are going to get hurt. We heal very slowly.

When we start bleeding, it's not just cantankerous senior officers we need to worry about. In fact, they are the least of our concerns. Our concerns are the enlisted soldiers who do not wear the wreath or chevrons. If they don't hold us in high esteem and trust us, what the hell good are we?

After all, without sounding too sappy about it, we are here for them—not them for us. When we forget that, it allows folks who never walked a step in an enlisted soldier's shoes to make such statements as, "There are damn few greater responsibilities than taking care of soldiers and preparing them for battle, and our newly exalted CSMs don't do these things." Or it lets them wonder out loud about what "the length of the CSM's leash" is.

So what is this 2 percent that jams a stake in the heart of the command sergeant major corps and subsequently the entire NCO corps? I hate to use their phrase, but it's the three Ps—perks, privileges, and politics. As a group, we are guilty as charged. If one of us does it, we are all guilty by association.

There isn't a command sergeant major alive today, active or retired, who doesn't know of someone getting an important assignment because of political connections rather than qualifications—politics. We also know those who accept things offered to them because of their position—perks. Some of us express a lot more concern about where we live than about where our soldiers live—privileges. On top of all that, too many of us spend more time looking for upwardly mobile jobs than focusing on doing the ones we have. Enough said?

Unfortunately, there are enough of us out there doing those kinds of things to cause many to form an untrue and undeserved opinion of us all. I think that becomes fairly obvious in articles such as the one I've been talking about.

If there are enough folks in the army who have such a negative opinion of command sergeants major, they will hold the same contempt for all noncommissioned officers. There is not much you can do to change the opinions held by some. Their own insecurities are usually the foundation of their opinions in the first place. What NCOs have to do is to ensure that when such opinions are put out for world consumption, whoever hears them can judge them for what they are.

We do that by projecting an accurate image of most noncommissioned officers. We have to emphasize a different set of Ps in everything we do—pride, professionalism, and performance. These are the foundation of the noncommissioned officers' creed. We don't need to look any further than that—and to the basic values of courage, candor, commitment, competence, and compassion— for the direction in which to lead the NCO corps.

Pride

I am proud of the corps of noncommissioned officers and will at all times conduct myself so as to bring credit upon the Corps, the Military Service and my country regardless of the situation in which I find myself. I will not use my grade or position to attain pleasure, profit, or personal safety. —*The NCO Creed*

Professionalism

No one is more professional than I. . . . Competence is my watchword. My two basic responsibilities will always be uppermost in my mind—accomplishment of my mission and the welfare of my soldiers. I will strive to remain tactically and technically proficient. I am aware of my role as a Noncommissioned Officer. I will fulfill my responsibilities inherent in that role. All soldiers are entitled to outstanding leadership; I will provide that leadership. I know my soldiers and I will always place their needs above my own. I will communicate consistently with my soldiers and never leave them uninformed. I will be fair and impartial when recommending both rewards and punishment. —*The NCO Creed*

Performance

Officers of my unit will have maximum time to accomplish their duties; they will not have to accomplish mine. I will earn their respect and confidence as well as that of my soldiers. I will be loyal to those with whom I serve; seniors, peers, and subordinates alike. I will exercise initiative by taking appropriate action in the absence of orders. I will not compromise my integrity, nor my moral courage, I will not forget, nor will I allow my comrades to forget that we are professionals, Noncommissioned Officers, leaders! —*The NCO Creed*

There's your direction. Any questions?

Give All You Can or Get All You Can?

It is more blessed to give than to receive.
—*Acts 25:35*

In his book *The Art of the Leader,* William A. Cohen discusses two games that organizations play. He describes the Get All You Can Game as one in which the leaders and members of the organization are more interested in personal gain than they are in making a contribution. He goes on to explain how this destroys cohesiveness, esprit de corps, and the effectiveness of the organization.

He describes the opposite as the Give All You Can Game. An organization that plays this game has leaders and members that are interested in what they can contribute to the organization, not what they can get out of it for themselves. Both games, Cohen says, originate with the leadership of the organizations.

I heard a story once. Two young men just out of high school got jobs working for the railroad. Twenty-five years after they started, one was the president of the railroad, and the other was still at the low-level job he had in the beginning.

One day someone asked the man with the low-level job why he never progressed, while his friend was able to move to the top of the organization, adding that his friend appeared to be no smarter than he. "It's simple," he responded. "Twenty-five years ago my friend went to work for the railroad. I went to work for a paycheck." In the army, we can also find leaders who work for paychecks and those who work for the army.

When leaders express more concern about where they live and how they are treated (the perks) than they do about their soldiers, they are breeding the Get All You Can mentality. It's a very destructive mentality for an organization. The army cannot survive without cohesion and esprit de corps—the first two casualties of the Get Game.

In an organization in which leaders practice Give All You Can, you'll find many examples of the army values, especially selfless service. Many other words come to mind to describe these organizations—teamwork, dedication, motivation, pride in work. . . . I think you get the point.

Give or Get? It's the simplest choice you can make, and it has the greatest impact on the soldiers and organizations you lead.

Leaders' Priorities

I know your works, love, service, faith and your patience; and as for your works, the last are more than the first. —*Revelations 2:19*

Successful leaders learn from their experiences. They use their knowledge of past weaknesses to strengthen themselves, their soldiers, and their units. From experience, they develop priorities and direction.

I have learned from the example set by some great non-commissioned officers. I have also learned from the example set by some pitiful noncommissioned officers. The great ones always had a sense of direction and a clear picture of where they were going. They had real priorities. The others never quite got the hang of that. The great soldiers knew history and relied on its lessons for priorities.

Every day, we improve what we do in the army by using history lessons called After Action Reviews and Lessons Learned. Knowing history will tell you where leaders and soldiers were when they developed their priorities. We have built a successful army because a lot of soldiers learned to rely on history for answers, direction, and priorities. I believe you have to understand your leaders as well as you understand those you are charged to lead. With that in mind, let's talk about our leaders and their priorities.

The senior leaders of our army today started their service between 1965 and 1970. Do you know where our army was in 1965? It was in the jungles of Southeast Asia, in a country a lot of the soldiers of the time had never heard of before. It was fighting and dying in a stifling hot, humid, and unforgiving jungle without a clear mission. It was in a war that the entire force had not been mobilized to support and that the American public was not behind. It was the victim of one-year rotations that dissolved the continuity of small-unit leadership that is so crucial to success.

The noncommissioned officer corps was caught in a loop of repeated rotations and combat tours. The strength of the middle-grade noncommissioned officer corps shrank to a state in which it couldn't meet the needs of the army. The bridge of noncommissioned officer leadership between soldiers and company-grade officers was almost gone. In many cases, officers performed roles that would traditionally belong to noncommissioned officers.

The middle-grade noncommissioned officers were technically competent, but lacked the years of leadership experience to which our soldiers and army were entitled and accustomed. These technically competent NCOs were the products of a noncommissioned officer candidate school designed to rapidly replenish the shortage of middle-grade noncommissioned officers. The products of this school were called Shake and Bakes. They were sergeants who were expected to lead soldiers in combat with as little as twenty-two weeks service in the army—men they didn't know before they arrived in Vietnam. Their experience included basic training, combat arms noncommissioned officer candidate school, and maybe one cycle each as assistant drill sergeant.

If you take a look at a sergeant first class promotion list today, you will see that it takes an average of thirteen years for a staff sergeant to make that list. This NCO typically will have spent five years as a staff sergeant and eight years at other ranks before that. He or she will spend another year or two on the list before being promoted.

The Shake and Bake program, on the other hand, gave us technically competent but young and inexperienced sergeants to lead eighteen- and nineteen-year-old privates. These sergeants answered to very young platoon sergeants who had received accelerated promotions. All were reporting to brand-new, inexperienced lieutenants and captains, also the benefactors of accelerated promotions.

This was the small-unit leadership soldiers had to rely on to help them survive combat against a professional and experienced enemy regular army and a force of seasoned guerilla fighters. They were fighting the same force that had defeated the elite French army at the battle of Dien Bien Phu only a few years earlier.

This is the era that produced the senior leaders of our army. These young, inexperienced NCOs and officers grew up to be senior leaders, whose priorities became training, leadership, and the professional development of the noncommissioned officer corps. They started the development of what is now the best noncommissioned officer education system in the world. These leaders, more than any others, understand the value of a strong, professionally developed and experienced noncommissioned officer corps.

The next group of army senior leaders is from the post-Vietnam 1970s. As military scholars will tell you, this was the period in our history during which the army that had once rolled back the Imperial Japanese Army, the Third Reich Wehrmacht, and the Communist Chinese in Korea was now broken.

It was called a hollow force—a paper army. It had inadequate training and worn-out, poorly maintained equipment and facilities. It was an army still reeling from its experience in Vietnam, which the American public continued to view as a poorly led collection of drug-addicted baby killers capable of producing another Mai Lai massacre. It was infested with slackers, drug abusers, and alcoholics.

We had a lot of undesirable soldiers and noncommissioned officers in that army. It called itself the new Volunteer Army, or VOLAR. Its recruiting theme was "The Army Wants to Join You." As a young private in that army in Korea, I watched senior noncommissioned officers, while leading by example, go through a ritual of shotgunning beers so they could stop shaking long enough to go to work in the morning. This ritual kept them steady until they could get to the club to have some more beers for lunch. Oh, it was accepted then. Having a few beers for lunch, that is. We even had beer machines in the mess hall.

This was the same army in which I spent thirteen months in Korea sitting in the middle of the traditional invasion route for the armies of the north, and never once participated in or observed an organized physical fitness training session. I never fired my weapon, even to zero it. I never had any survival skills training and was never issued or fitted with a protective mask. The highlight of the day was happy hour at the club, where the goal was to consume all the alcohol you could while the drinks were half-price.

It was a time when the smell of burning marijuana permeated the barracks. It was also a time when a handful of pills, purchased from some shady character in an alley in the village, was a morning ritual for another group of soldiers.

The leaders who brought our army out of that dark period in its history, to their great credit, are senior leaders in our army today. These senior soldiers' priorities are training, discipline, adherence to standards, and a high state of soldier and equipment readiness. These are the leaders who built the ground force that devastated the fourth-largest standing army in the world in just 100 hours. They simply refused to let their army continue in the state in which they inherited it. These leaders also learned the hard way how to properly draw an army down. They learned the lessons of their time very well.

The soldiers who will be the senior leaders of Force XXI (the army with which we'll start the twenty-first century) are our first generation of high-technology soldiers from the 1980s. I call them "Nintendo, want-it-right-now" soldiers. They have been exposed to high technology most of their lives. In fact, it is the way of life they have come to know. That's why they will readily accept the high-technology personality and challenges of Force XXI.

The fear I have for this group relates to their sometimes impatient approach. To paraphrase some training I had once, they have repeatedly seen complex problems solved during sitcoms that lasted thirty minutes—including light beer and "just do it" commercials. They have seen Chuck Norris and Sylvester Stallone solve the Vietnam MIA problem, commercially uninterrupted, in ninety minutes.

What this group cannot allow itself to forget is that the leaders who took them through Desert Storm evacuated Saigon twenty years earlier vowing to never again go to war without a clear mission, a well-trained and well-equipped force, and the wherewithal to fight, win, and survive. They were successful because they remembered the lessons they learned early, and they rebuilt their army with patience.

During the 1980s, the finest noncommissioned officer education system in the world nearly completed its evolution. Our noncommissioned officers became thoroughly schooled in battle-focused training doctrine and came to clearly understand their role in training. Senior noncommissioned officers were trained in the highest levels of military operations. They became educated in the principles of war and the tenets of our air-land battle doctrine, not so they could perform officer functions as some detractors have suggested, but so they were better equipped to give the army the trained soldiers it needed.

The soldiers of the 1980s were the benefactors of the system and doctrine built by the soldiers of the post-Vietnam 1970s. These soldiers knew what was lacking in the army they inherited, and they knew what was needed to produce an effective army and noncommissioned officer corps. With patience, hard work, and craftsmanship, they did it. That is the most important lesson the future senior leaders of Force XXI must remember.

Now we come to the noncommissioned officers of the 1990s. In a few years, you will inherit the leadership of the only true superpower army on the face of the earth. You will lead in what's called "The Army After Next." What will be your legacy? You will be the first NCO corps that grew up in a U.S.-based force projection army.

Learn the lessons of your predecessors, who spent half their careers in other countries. You are the corps that will respond often to short-notice contingency operations and to operations other than war, such as disaster relief, drug interdiction, and peacekeeping. Remember the lessons learned by your predecessors about training and soldier and equipment readiness. There is a small resurgence of drug abuse in the army; learn the lessons of your predecessors in aggressively dealing with that problem.

You are the corps on the front end of quality-of-life changes that will completely change how soldiers live in garrison. Your predecessors never experienced that. Get it right so that your successors can learn from you. You will be leading a highly technical force, in which one soldier replaces many and probably does so more effectively.

You are inheriting a great army. Your major challenge is to not become a noncommissioned officer corps known for complacency and for allowing our army to return to the state it was in twenty years ago. Learn the lessons of history, and continue to direct the noncommissioned corps and our army toward the twenty-first century. Remember this quote from Gen. John A. Wickham, Jr., former army chief of staff:

> Make a difference. The time each of us is in charge is short. By leaving things better than they were, you will be making history in the army.

Noncommissioned Officers Are Team Builders

> Leadership can be defined in numerous ways, but probably the simplest definition is that leadership in any unit revolves around the ability of the person in charge to move a group of people, as a team, in the direction of a common goal. —Department of the Army Pamphlet 600-65, *November 1985, author unknown*

Many things in the army are certain. The most certain of all is that the army is not an individual experience. It is made of teams of all sizes. Without effective teams, the army fails. Of all the challenges facing a noncommissioned officer, none is more important than building a team. The foundation of a successful unit is cohesive and effective teams sharing a common goal—a common direction.

When I was a drill sergeant, I had a platoon that was different from any I'd had before. In about the third week of training, a line of trainees was standing at my door at the end of every training day. They didn't come to talk about personal problems, which was the norm. They came to complain about one another. When I walked into the platoon bay, I'd find them isolated in their personal areas, barely even talking. For whatever reason, they were not coming together as a team.

The most difficult parts of the training cycle were still to come, and many of these soldiers, without peer instruction and encouragement from their platoon mates, simply would not make it. Realizing that, I dug into my toolbox and pulled out a little teamwork exercise I had learned. I told the trainees that the platoon had been gigged by the first sergeant during morning inspection for sloppily made bunks. (As any drill sergeant can tell you, that statement could be true on any day.) Because of that, we were going to learn to make bunks like we did on the first day of basic training.

Step by step, I explained to them how to make a bed the right way. They performed each step as I talked. I could see by the expressions on their faces and some rolling eyes that they believed they were beyond this point in their training. As individuals, they were. After we had our class, I told them to strip their bunks to the mattress covers; we were going to practice. I told them that when I blew my whistle, they were to begin making their beds, and the second time I blew it, they were to stop. I would always blow the whistle before anyone had a chance to finish and make them start over.

After about fifteen minutes, some of them realized that they could never get their bunks made alone. So, in pairs and even in threes, they began working on their beds together. Of course, as soon as I saw them doing this, I made sure the teams had time to complete the task. Eventually, a team formed to make every bed in the bay. I never suggested to them that they form teams. It became obvious to them that their only hope for completing the task was to use teams. Teamwork was never an issue with this platoon again. They finished the cycle as the honor platoon.

The team is the basis for everything a unit does. Noncommissioned officers must master team building. Team building goes much deeper than bunk-making drills. The bunk drill was a tool that demonstrated to the trainees that they needed one another to reach the common goal, and that individuals acting alone can never accomplish what a team can. When a soldier understands the need for a cohesive unit team, the other aspects of team building are more easily overcome.

A drill sergeant's perspective on the parade field and the soldiers on it during a graduation review paints a vivid picture of the huge team-building challenge faced by noncommissioned officers. It also lays out the many variables noncommissioned officers must overcome to mold a collection of individuals into an effective team pointed toward a common goal. It highlights the importance of instilling the teamwork mentality into soldiers. Teamwork is the first and most important lesson that soldiers must learn, and that noncommissioned officers must teach them.

Here is that drill sergeant's perspective:

He was impressed, standing there in front of them, with how clean, tall, and straight they looked. Although there was a slight breeze causing their coattails and trouser legs to flap about, they were, for the most part, motionless. Rigid may be a better term. Most were putting forth special effort to ensure they remained so. Their pride, accented with a touch of arrogance, was obvious. It was, for some of them, their first real accomplishment. For others, not here now, it had been a continuation of lifelong failures.

This position was not unfamiliar to him. He had been here often. Still, as he faced about and put his back to them, that same arrogant pride was radiating from him. Again, as it always did, the sound of the national anthem caused a tingling in the pit of his stomach and a shiver to race down his back. During the usual string of speeches, which always seemed to be the same, his mind started to wander.

Two months ago, they had arrived. They were a true assortment of people. The expression he remembered from his training was "a cross-section of our society." Some of them were fat and some were not. Some of them were smart and some were not so smart. Some were lazy and some were not. Some were, or had been, poor, and some were not. Some were there because they had to be, some were there because they wanted to be, and others were there because they did not know what they wanted.

They came from all compass points. Some were from the city and some were definitely not from the city. Some were black and some were white. Some were neither black nor white. Some of them were frightened and some were not. Most were cautious and uncertain. All they really had in common was being in the same place, at the same time, and for the same reason. They wanted to be soldiers.

His job—and he was good at it—was to give them what they wanted. For two months he taught, conditioned, and drilled them until they performed as one, in unison, to his commands. He watched them succeed and fail. He watched them transform from an odd lot into a team that encouraged, helped, and supported each other. Now it was time to send them away. He wondered, as he always did, if he had supplied them with the necessary tools to continue being successful.

The Alabama sun was getting warmer. The grass parade field and humidity combined to make it uncomfortable. He knew that in a matter of hours they would be gone, and forty new faces, with old problems, would replace them. He had once stood where they were now standing, so he knew their thoughts. They were uncertain about the future. Some did not want to leave the close relationships they had developed. Others were ready for the next adventure. All, however, were soldiers.

When he faced about, they were still there, as he had known they would be. They were still rigid. The sun had taken a little of the arrogance out of their expressions, but they were still proud. They were soldiers. He knew when he marched them past the reviewing stand that they would be the best. Graduating from army basic training was something they would only do once. After two months of hard work, he was confident that they would get this part right the first time.

The Truth Is . . .

I never give them hell. I just tell the truth, and they think it's hell. —*Harry S. Truman*

Everyone needs to have some things they hold to be the truth: truth that applies to every situation and never changes. Universal truth, some philosophers call it. I have some truths of my own invention and others I've picked up along the way and adopted. All of them help me understand where I'm coming from and also where I'm going. It might be a good idea if you come up with some of your own. Feel free to borrow some of these.

The truth is:

Most luck is a product of hard work. Winning the lottery isn't; getting promoted is.

Your rank is an indicator of your pay grade, not your leadership ability. Any questions?

Average doesn't count. Everybody remembers who came in first place and who the criminals were. So if fame is what you're after, you need to figure out which end of the spectrum appeals to you; then go there.

There will always be somebody who hates your guts. Make sure you know who it is.

Enforce the standard and you never have to explain what you did. Standards and rules are there for a reason; enforce them.

Soldiers create the environment in which they want to live. When you tell soldiers the standard of performance expected of them, their mission, and the consequences of success and failure, they will make a conscious choice about what they want to pursue. They'll choose the environment they want to be in.

A little Pfc. work never hurt anybody. Sometimes you need to roll your sleeves up.

Sometimes the words you have to say need to hit the recipient in the head like a rock to get his or her attention. Say what's on your mind so you don't think later about what you should have said.

Most good noncommissioned officers operate from a basic philosophy. Some officers and an occasional lawyer even understand it. If you don't want an honest, frank answer supported by facts, don't ask them any questions. If you don't want a standard enforced, don't write it into a regulation.

If you insist that it is not possible to do something and then you find someone doing it, you should leave him or her the hell alone.

The possibility of failure comes with risk taking. Otherwise, it would be called sure-thing taking. Sometimes you have to take a chance.

You should stop complaining about the people you

don't have and figure out what you can do with the people you do have.

According to Sergeant Major of the Army Connelly, "It is difficult to be a good noncommissioned officer. If it had been easy, they would have given it to the officer corps."

Some people like to listen to themselves talk. I think you ought to let them.

People who say, "If I were you I'd . . ." probably wouldn't if they were you.

You need to make sure you have the whole story. Or, as Huck Finn put it, "Well, ther ain't no sense in it, a body might stump his toe, and take pison, and fall down the well, and break his neck and bust his brains out, and somebody come along and ask what killed him and some numskull up and say, 'Why, he stumped his toe.' Would there be any sense in that?"

You should never try to teach a pig how to sing. It wastes your time and annoys the pig. Don't teach useless tasks to your soldiers, either.

Learning about the past is OK, but wallowing in it isn't. "This looks just like another Vietnam. . . ."

You need to know who you are and what you do, and stay focused on that.

A porcupine with its quills down is just another fat rodent.

Success

Be of the same mind toward one another. Do not set your mind on high things, but associate with the humble. Do not be wise in your own opinion.
—*Romans 12:16*

When I decided to stay in the army, my goal was to become a hard-stripe noncommissioned officer. For me, that was the rank of staff sergeant. It equaled success and opened a lot of doors. My success was short-lived, because my goals started moving. Success became the next rank or assignment. I had to become a drill sergeant. Then not just any drill sergeant, but the senior drill sergeant. After that, I had to be a first sergeant. Being a first sergeant, I thought, would be enough. As a first sergeant, it wasn't long before I knew I would have to be promoted to command sergeant major to feel successful.

After becoming a command sergeant major and being assigned to a battalion, I wondered about the possibility of someday working at higher levels, maybe even for a general officer. Then I started thinking: When does this obsession with success end? Only one of us at a time will ever be the sergeant major of the army. Should the rest of us feel like failures if we never get past a battalion?

The odds against becoming a command sergeant major are astronomical. It's probably about the same as a football player making it to the Super Bowl. Maybe someone should do the math one day. Is every soldier who doesn't make command sergeant major a failure? Is every football player who doesn't make it to the Super Bowl a failure? I don't think so. But I suppose that depends on what you consider success.

By whose definition are we successful? By what standard is success measured? When does a person know he or she is a success? Are there different levels of success? Just what exactly is success, and how do you get there from here? Tough questions? Yes, they are, and each deserves a thorough, complex answer. But I'm not sure I have one. Do you?

Success has as many different definitions and means of achieving it as there are people to ask. If it's that hard to arrive at an acceptable definition of success, how do we know when we are successful?

When we see a $500,000 house, with matching Mercedes SL 500s in the driveway, tennis courts, and an in-ground pool in the backyard, we think, "success." Pete Rose's hitting record and Cal Ripken's consecutive game streak, to most of us, equal success. When we think about Bill Gates's billions, naturally, we think, "success."

What about the common folks? Can a garbage collector, street sweeper, or truck driver be a success? By the standards most of us attach to success, the answer is no. That nagging question once again is: By whose standard is a person successful? Is this success thing we push toward all our lives measured by material possessions, billions of dollars, or some other achievement—the rank insignia on our collars or the number of ribbons on our chests?

The expression "visible success" certainly leads us to that conclusion. The Mercedes in the driveway, Rose's and Ripken's records, and Gates's billions are visible signs of success. Do you reckon any of our blue-collar folks will ever have those visible indicators of success? Ha!

Does success have to be visible? Is it necessary to walk around with a placard hanging on your chest saying, "Hey, I'm a success! Didn't you see my picture on the front of *Money* magazine?" We wear our success in the army. The ranks on our sleeves and the awards hanging on our chests are visible indicators of success.

I don't want to disappoint all of you visibly successful folks. Well, yeah I do. Real success is not visible. It has nothing to do with the size of your house, your batting average, or your bank account, or in our case, the number of medals you've managed to get. Those things are OK, granted. But success is how you feel every day. It's being satisfied with the day's work you've produced. It's feeling at ease with yourself when you go home at night.

You see, Cal, Pete, and Bill may never be successful. Their mindset may never allow them to be satisfied with a day's work. Sure, they'll have all the outward signs of success. What they may never do, though, is reach an end. In their minds, they may never be successful because they may never sit down and say, "This is where I stop. When I get here, I'm a success." Success is elusive to them because their endpoint keeps moving.

In the army, a lot of my command sergeant major peers suffer from this complex. They spend their lives trying to become command sergeants major, against incredible odds. Then, as command sergeants major, they believe they are not successful unless they are working for general officers. Their success points keep moving. It gets very foggy when they begin to concentrate on upward mobility instead of their jobs and their already successful careers. That's another issue, though.

Our garbage collector, on the other hand, is a total success. He knows his goal today is to complete his rounds. When he's accomplished that, he is successful. When he goes home tonight he will be at ease, realizing that his goals for today were met. He was a success. He won't think about tomorrow's business until tomorrow, when he will be a success again.

Success is something that's internalized. Unless a success goal is clearly established in our minds, we can't ever get there. Did Cal have a success goal? If it was to break the record, then he would have quit when that happened. But now, every day is a new record. When do we quit? I think if Pete were still in the game, they would be rolling him out to the plate to pinch-hit from a wheelchair, just so he could add one more to the record. And Bill. Just how many billions does one person need?

The garbage collector is the only success of the bunch. He completes the task at hand every day. No matter how tiny that may be to Bill, Pete, and Cal, it's success for him. He'll probably live longer, too, provided he can afford health insurance.

A successful NCO will know what his or her daily goals are, and will never judge the success of another based on some supposed visible indicator of success.

Summary

- A noncommissioned officer uses personal battle focus to be in control of his or her life. The NCO applies the principles of battle-focused training to leading his or her life in the right direction. You must develop a personal mission, a vision, essential tasks, a means of assessing where you are, and a plan to get you where you want to be.
- Leaders must always have direction for themselves and those they are charged to lead. Leaders establish direction for themselves by knowing what good leaders do and what qualities they must project.

- Noncommissioned officers must focus on the three Ps for direction: pride, performance, and professionalism.
- Leaders establish direction and priorities for their units by knowing history and carrying its lessons with them into the future.
- A leader can choose to be a Give leader or a Get leader. Give leaders build cohesive teams and organizations that live the value of selfless service.
- The most important and challenging thing for a leader to do is to build a team out of a diverse group of people and focus them toward the common goal of the unit.
- A leader must operate within a personal set of guiding principles or truths. By doing so, you build consistency, and your soldiers will always know where you are coming from.
- Leaders establish goals that always allow them to define success for themselves and their units.

CHAPTER THREE
BEING THE EXAMPLE

Noncommissioned officers (NCOs) must never forget that they are the model soldiers imitate. Their approach to being NCOs and soldiers, good or bad, will be copied. Consciously or not, they will be the example.

Stay in Your Lane

Sometimes, and for any number of reasons, noncommissioned officers get off track and fail to meet their responsibilities to soldiers. The most important thing NCOs do is take care of soldiers.

First Sergeant Pedro Olivari was an influential role model for me. He spoke with a heavy accent, but, like others, I always listened intently. He had received a battlefield commission during the Korean War, achieved the rank of captain, and become a company commander. A reduction in force gave him the option of leaving the army or becoming a sergeant again. To the army's good fortune, he chose the latter.

He was proud of the time he had spent as an officer, but was quick to let us know how serious he was about being a sergeant. He had trained, cared for, and led soldiers in peace and combat, both as an officer and as a sergeant.

His perspective on soldiering was unique and valuable. His advice was tested and sound. He knew his lane.

Top Olivari wasn't the recruiting-poster image that you may be painting in your mind. Instead, he was about five-foot-six and barrel-chested. A stubby cigar was his constant companion.

He was prone to doing things that were unheard of in 1972. Every night, for example, alone and wearing canvas sneakers, he would run about five laps around the perimeter of Camp Red Cloud, Korea. He did this at a time when the focus on physical fitness in the army was not at the forefront. I haven't seen Camp Red Cloud in a number of years, but in 1972, that was a pretty good run.

The most vivid memories I have of Olivari mentoring soldiers and officers involve us standing around the diesel space heater in the Quonset hut that served as the Headquarters and Headquarters Company (HHC), I Corps, orderly room.

Usually, some section sergeants and sometimes a lieutenant or two stopped off there after morning formation. Olivari never kept his own office; he just had a desk out front beside the company's clerk. There was a room he could have used, but for whatever reason, he never did.

Olivari's morning usually consisted of going over his duty roster meticulously with red and blue pencils, looking at the charge-of-quarters (CQ) duty journal, and just listening. One morning, after listening for a while to some sergeants complaining about an officer who they didn't think was doing his job very well, Olivari got into one of his counseling sessions.

His movements were always the same and served as a signal to everyone that something was coming. He would get up from his desk, saunter over to the heater, and stand directly across from the most vocal individual there. He would hold his hands out and rub them together over the stove for a few seconds.

Then he would take the cigar stub out of the corner of his mouth. Holding it between his thumb and forefinger and using his remaining three fingers like a pointer, he would always start by saying, "My son"—which was how he addressed everyone.

This particular morning he told the sergeant, "My son, if you want to make it in this army, you'd better spend your time worrying about your soldiers and how you do your job. You have to know what you are supposed to do and then do it. Don't waste your time worrying about how an officer does his job. That's the officer's business. If your soldiers fail, it won't be an officer's fault." What he was telling that sergeant was, "Stay in your lane."

Another time, after listening to a sergeant's complaints about his soldiers being more interested in going to the clubs in the village than they were in doing their jobs— and going through his choreographed steps—he said, "My son, soldiers go where their sergeants lead them."

I observed and was the benefactor of many of these counseling sessions. Lately, I have had reason to reflect on just how solid Pedro Olivari's advice still is.

In every facet of our lives, whether social or professional, before, during, or after the army, we always have a specific role to play. We always have a lane in which to operate. In team sports we have a position to play—a lane.

If we get out of our lane and into another's, the team breaks down, and if we continue to operate out of our lane, the team fails.

In our profession, we're obligated to fulfill our roles by providing leadership to our junior soldiers, and the proper example for them to follow. Put simply in everything we do, we have to clearly define our lane and stay in it. We have to know its boundaries and all the challenges that lie within those boundaries. If we fail to meet the challenges that are in our lane, our team will break down and ultimately fail.

If you know your lane, staying in it is easy. When NCOs are in the structure of a platoon, squad, or team, the lane boundaries and all that is in the lane are usually clear to them. A lot of sergeants, finding themselves in an environment with less structure, sometimes lose focus of what their lane is.

Our lane of responsibility is spelled out for us in *Army Regulation 600-20, Army Command Policy,* Chapter 3, "Enlisted Aspects of Command." The sum of these responsibilities equals taking care of soldiers.

Taking care of soldiers means counseling and knowing them, training them to standards, enforcing discipline, and setting an example for them to emulate. These responsibilities never waver and are always in our lane regardless of our mission.

They are the same for a sergeant in charge of soldiers in a personnel service center as they are for a sergeant in charge of soldiers in an infantry platoon. Soldier care responsibilities do not change with your mission; they are constant.

Above and before all else, we have to remember we are sergeants. It's when we start calling ourselves senior enlisted advisors or the noncommissioned officers in charge (NCOIC) of something or other that our lanes start to get a little unclear.

In other words, when we refer to ourselves as job descriptions instead of sergeants, we start losing track of who we are and what we do. By forgetting that we are sergeants before we are anything else, we narrow our lane or focus too much. When that happens, the most important obligation and responsibility in our lane—taking care of soldiers—falls out of it.

Recently, I asked an NCOIC to tell me what exactly it was he was in charge of. He answered with a detailed briefing that included the section's mission, how it was accomplished, and how well it was accomplished, measured by the Department of the Army standard for accomplishing that particular mission. During the briefing he never mentioned his responsibilities, as a sergeant, to the soldiers in the section.

I was impressed with his job knowledge. When I asked him about taking care of soldiers, however, his answers were not given with the same zeal as was his mission briefing. I asked questions about things that are in the NCO lane of responsibility defined in *Army Regulation 600-20*.

I asked about counseling. The answer offered was a recital of his unit's policy on counseling. When I asked to see one of his counseling records, he couldn't produce one because counseling wasn't being done. When I asked about physical training, he told me, "Because of the constraints of our mission, we do it on our own." Doing it on their own meant that privates now had the responsibility to develop and maintain adequate physical fitness programs—something a lot of sergeants have difficulty with.

The sergeant had pushed a soldier care responsibility, which was plainly his, out of his lane. I asked the sergeant what happened if one of his soldiers failed the physical fitness test or became overweight. His reply was, "The first sergeant takes care of that."

Now the sergeant was pushing responsibility out of his lane and into the first sergeant's. There were more questions with similar replies during our discussion. When our talk was over, the sergeant had cleared his lane of soldier care responsibilities. Too many times, the responsibility was placed in the soldiers' lane, or forgotten altogether.

I have faced this situation in garrison and line units. I find it's not peculiar to one or the other. It's a clear example of a sergeant forgetting who he is and what he does. By neglecting his soldier care responsibilities, this sergeant wandered out of his lane and into an officer's lane.

Officers have a different focus—another lane. Their main focus is the mission at hand, and they concentrate on the collective picture. They do that because they know that the sergeants shoulder the responsibility to provide them with trained and cared-for soldiers to accomplish the mission.

Our failure to meet that responsibility violates our creed and breaks down the team. Our soldiers lose confidence in us, our support channel breaks down, and officers pick up the soldier care responsibility we have neglected. When that happens, we scream like banshees because some officer is meddling in sergeants' business.

Before we do that, though, we need to make sure we are not the cause of the officer being in our lane in the first place. As NCOs, it is our responsibility not only to take care of soldiers, but also to help other sergeants define and stay in their lanes. If we allow taking care of soldiers to drop out of our lane, think about what lesson we are teaching tomorrow's sergeants. Tomorrow's sergeants are those whom we will charge to look after our sons and daughters.

Remember: "My son, soldiers go where sergeants lead them. Stay in your lane, Sergeant."

The Mirror Image

One of my three-meter-zone mentors told me, "When you look at soldiers, you see yourself. If you ever do something dumb, you'll see it again."

General George Patton added a different perspective to this thought: "Soldiers, all men in fact, are natural hero worshippers. Officers with a flare for command realize this and emphasize in their conduct, dress, and deportment the qualities they seek to produce in their men. . . ."

Just as we have to always think about the expectations our soldiers have for us, we must always be conscious of the model we provide for our soldiers. To soldiers, leaders represent success. Soldiers mimic success by following the examples of their successful leaders. Our rank represents to soldiers that we have done the right things to get where we are.

It doesn't matter if you are the youngest command sergeant major in the army or the oldest sergeant rapidly approaching your retention control point. Young soldiers are impressionable, and they will follow your example. Just as children mimic adults they are close to, young soldiers will mimic their closest leaders. They will become the mirror image of the leaders in their three-meter zones.

Whether you like it or not, you are on display at all times. Your actions say much more than your words. Subordinates will watch carefully and imitate your behavior. You must accept the obligation to be a worthy role model and you cannot ignore the effect your behavior has on others.   Field Manual 22-100, *1990*

Noncommissioned officers live in a fishbowl. Soldiers constantly watch and copy everything we do. The more senior we are, the larger our fishbowl and our sphere of influence over soldiers become. They want to be where we are, wearing the rank we are wearing and enjoying the prestige and privilege that come with it. Soldiers will pick up our bad habits as well as our good ones. We represent success to them, and we lead by example twenty-four hours a day.

When you look at your section, squad, platoon, or whatever it is you are leading, you are looking into a mirror. Check the appearance of your soldiers. If they look sloppy, you need to take a long, hard look at your own appearance. Look at the performance of your soldiers. Do they suffer from D-minus syndrome? If they have an average physical fitness test score of 180 points (D-minus syndrome), re-examine your own fitness practices. We could continue with this, but I expect you get the point.

Just as soldiers mirror their leaders, units mirror their NCO corps. In any unit, there is a key NCO who sets the tone for how the rest of the NCOs perform and, subsequently, how the soldiers of the unit view them. In a company, it's the first sergeant. The first sergeant, the six of diamonds, is the most powerful and influential soldier in the army. He or she is the model for the rest of the noncommissioned officers and soldiers in the unit. That's why the first sergeant is called "Top." First sergeants are the top soldiers in their units.

If you doubt the influence of a unit first sergeant, find a unit, any unit, and look at the soldiers and noncommissioned officers of the unit before you meet the first sergeant. Odds are, you will have an accurate impression of the first sergeant before you meet him or her. You'll know what to expect because you have been looking in the first sergeant's mirror. A first sergeant who has a poor bearing and appearance, weak fitness habits, and a bad work ethic, and who comes up short on candor, courage, competence, commitment, and compassion, will mold platoon sergeants and section sergeants into his or her mirror image.

Platoon sergeants and section leaders, in turn, mold squad leaders, team leaders, and other first-line NCOs into their mirror images. Soldiers in the entire unit then become the mirror image of their NCO corps or, more specifically, its first sergeant.

Using the illustration of the unit, it becomes easy to figure out how the army is a mirror image of its noncommissioned officer corps. Every noncommissioned officer has a sphere of influence—his or her mirror. It's a process that leaves no NCO leader untouched and, as an extension, no soldier untouched.

NCOs have to be aware of where their most important influence is. They need to be aware of their mirror, their sphere of influence—their three-meter zone. For example, a battalion command sergeant major can easily gauge his or her performance by looking to the first sergeants in the battalion. They are the command sergeant major's mirror.

There is a lot of truth to the claim we make to being the backbone of the army. Whether it's a straight, strong, and healthy backbone supporting a strong army or a weak, crippled one holding up a weak army is wholly dependent on noncommissioned officers realizing the influence they have over it. The army is a mirror image of the noncommissioned officer corps. Your little piece of it is a mirror image of you.

Expectations

When you become a noncommissioned officer, constantly remind yourself that you are the example soldiers follow. Whether you are driving down the road, doing physical training, buying milk at the store, or at work, you are the example. Soldiers watch you all the time. Soldiers are watching to see if you live up to their expectations of what a noncommissioned officer should be. They have the same expectations you had before you became a noncommissioned officer.

> [Soldiers] are looking at you when they must and, perhaps more importantly, when you don't expect it.
> —*Gen. John A. Wickham, Jr.*

We all have expectations. When people fail to live up to our expectations, our opinion of them is lowered. Others view us the same way.

Baron Frederick Wilhelm von Steuben established expectations for noncommissioned officers at the birth of our army with this guidance on their selection:

> The choice of noncommissioned officers is an object of the greatest importance: The order and discipline of a regiment depends so much upon their behavior, that too much care cannot be taken in preferring none to that trust but those who by their merit and good conduct are entitled to it. Honesty, sobriety, and a remarkable attention to every point of duty, with a neatness in their dress, are indispensable requisites; a spirit to command respect and obedience from the men, an expertness in performing every part of the exercise, are also absolutely necessary; nor can a sergeant or corporal be said to be qualified who does not write and read in a tolerable manner.

Field Manual 22-100, in its preface, says that army leaders must learn to fulfill the expectations of all soldiers, including other leaders. Those fundamental expectations laid out for leaders are to demonstrate tactical and technical competence; teach subordinates; be a good listener; treat soldiers with dignity and respect; stress basics; set the example; and set and enforce standards.

As youngsters, when we played soldier, everybody wanted to be the sergeant. I don't think we even considered that the army had another rank. The sergeant, to us, represented everything a soldier was supposed to be. To be anything else was settling for being less than the best.

Soldiers have expectations of what noncommissioned officers ought to be. This is partly because we boldly share our creed with them. We tell them that no one is more professional than we are. We state emphatically that we are leaders of soldiers and lay claim to being the backbone of the army. Uppermost in our minds, we tell them, are accomplishment of the mission and the welfare of our soldiers. These are lofty expectations that we pass to soldiers.

Adding to the expectation that we will live up to our creed is the mental image soldiers have of a sergeant. It's an image borne in the person of an always-spit-shined, always-pressed, always-firm, always-fair, and always-having-the-right-answers drill sergeant.

When we fail to live up to those great expectations, soldiers' opinions of us are lowered. General Omar Bradley expressed his and the American soldiers' expectations of noncommissioned officers like this:

> The noncommissioned officer wearing the chevron is supposed to be the best soldier in the platoon, and he is supposed to know how to perform all the duties expected of him. The American soldier expects his sergeant to be able to teach him how to do his job."

Soldiers' expectations change. Their expectations for squad leaders are different from their expectations for platoon sergeants. The higher the rank of an NCO, the higher soldiers' expectations are. Some soldiers' expectations for leaders are not realistic, but they are still their expectations. Soldiers know when leaders try to meet their expectations, and they form their opinions of them based on that.

Failure to live up to expectations can also cause soldiers to form low opinions of entire groups of people. If a soldier observes a military policeman intentionally breaking the law, for example, that soldier's opinion of all military policemen may be lowered. If a soldier gets bad service from one person at the clinic, the soldier's opinion of all the people at the clinic may be affected. If he or she has a bad experience with one bad NCO, his or her opinion of all NCOs may be affected.

When a noncommissioned officer meets the expectations of soldiers, it has a tremendously positive effect on individual soldiers and units. The following quote, attributed to an anonymous soldier and extracted from *Department of the Army Pamphlet 600-65*, vividly depicts that.

> If any of my sons are ever called upon to serve their country in time of war, I hope they will have a squad leader like I have. A true soldier, he's tough and demanding yet always fair. He cares about his squad. He sets high standards and demands that we meet them. He tells us what we do good and encourages us to keep our stuff straight. And he tells us what's screwed up and how to fix it. He knows as much about us and our families as is humanly possible. He truly cares.

We trust him and are confident in his ability to lead us in combat. If he says "follow me"—we will not hesitate. That's what leadership is all about.

Just as soldiers have expectations about what NCOs should look like and act like and how they should perform their duties, the same holds true for other ranks. Every squad leader has expectations of every platoon sergeant. Every platoon sergeant has expectations of every first sergeant. Every first sergeant has expectations of every command sergeant major.

The secret is to take expectations and turn them into success. It's not a complicated process. Write down your expectations. Commit them to memory. Otherwise, being human, you'll forget what they were when you reach that next-higher rank. Let the expectations you have for your leader become your standard for performance.

Each of us is led; some of us are leaders. The competence we demand in our leaders must be our model when we lead. —*Gen. Glen K. Otis*

Don't give up on your expectations. As a first sergeant, you were convinced your expectations of the command sergeant major were valid and realistic. Remember those thoughts you had? "If I were the command sergeant major, I'd . . ."

When you *are* the command sergeant major, the expectations you had as a first sergeant will be just as valid and realistic. You may not be able to live up to them, but you still have to try. Because, you see, expectations equal what we believe the perfect command sergeant major, first sergeant, platoon sergeant, or squad leader is. Just because living up to your expectations may be a little tougher than you bargained for does not make them invalid. Keep those expectations in your mind and constantly revisit them. Without even thinking about it, you will always work to achieve them. You are what you think you are, and you'll achieve what you think you'll achieve.

Soldiers have expectations of leaders. Leaders also have expectations of soldiers. The difference is that a soldier will never say, "Listen up, leader, here are my expectations of you." A leader, however, must tell a soldier what the expectations are. Personal expectations can never be too high because they represent your own image of an ideal performance. Expectations for soldiers, though, must always be realistic and attainable.

When you give your expectations to soldiers, leave room for them to excel. Your expectations have to be attainable for most soldiers, and they have to be at a level that can be surpassed by some. Never put a cap on your expectations of soldiers. Don't assign a maximum or a quitting point, and don't give out medals for reaching the minimum. Make sure your soldiers know that the minimum represents the floor of your expectations, not the ceiling. The minimum is a D-minus, barely passing. The maximum is an A. Exceeding the maximum is an A-plus. We always look for A-plus soldiers. Soldiers grade us the same way and are always looking for leaders who set an A-plus example. Count on it.

Don't Be an "I" Guy

A leader is best when people barely know he exists—
not so good when people obey and acclaim him.
Worse when they despise him. But of a good leader,
who talks little, when his work is done—his aim ful-
filled, they will say: "We did it ourselves." —*Lao Tzu*

"I took this unit when it was flat on its butt. I improved
its physical fitness test average, I improved its operational
readiness rate, I improved its barracks, I improved its
training," and on and on and on.

We have all heard these lines before. So have many,
many hardworking soldiers. And just like those hardworking soldiers, we kind of wonder, "What the hell were
the rest of us doing while you were getting everything
fixed?" Give credit where it's due. Don't be an "I" guy.

A leader stands out front and readily takes responsibility when things go wrong. In our profession, a line can usually be drawn from the failure directly back to the leader.

When things go wrong in your command, start
searching for the reason in increasingly larger con-
centric circles around your own desk.
—*Gen. Bruce Clarke*

That is a tremendous burden to tote around, but it
comes with the turf. As quickly as you accept ownership
of the failure of your unit, you must just as quickly pass
credit to those who did the work when things turn out
well. That's how a leader builds a loyal team.

"I probably told the unit's NCOs that we needed to improve our PT test average, but I probably didn't evaluate the first soldier one on one and help improve that score."

"I probably never turned one wrench in the motor pool to improve that OR rate."

"I never slapped one brushstroke of paint on those barracks that were improved, and I probably never got cheek to cheek with one soldier on the firing line to help raise his qualification score."

Do you get the point?

The soldiers and NCOs we depend on will always determine whether we are successes or failures. Any decent noncommissioned officer can identify many potential improvements that can be made in a unit, but can personally make very few of them. Soldiers, who turn the wrenches, slap the paint on the walls, and get that firing line dirt on their knees, need and deserve full credit for every success in a unit.

It is a given that leadership identifies problems and develops plans to fix them. But a plan is usually just a good-looking piece of paper until someone on the ground or in the motor pool executes it. More often than not, soldiers will take our shaky plans and turn them into something good anyway. Give credit where the work is done. Don't be an "I" guy, or the second time around, you may be saying, "I really don't know where I went wrong; it looked like such a good plan."

Acting Your Age

In our youth, our hearts were touched with fire.
—*Oliver Wendell Holmes*

It's the day after Thanksgiving. I still have sore legs, a sore back, and a sore neck, but they're getting better. My wife tells me if I learned to act my age, I wouldn't have these kinds of problems. What she is referring to are the two flag football games I played with young soldiers the day before Thanksgiving. I wasn't the only old codger on my pick-up team. There were a couple of commanders and at least one more command sergeant major. (Sorry about that hamstring thing, Sam. You know what happens to old legs when they get cold. You'll be off those crutches in a few days. Maybe you ought to learn to act your age.)

We did well, though, for codgers. We finished second in the Turkey Bowl football tournament. But we achieved something much more significant than that in the eyes of the young soldiers with whom we played. We showed them that biological age does not always equal physical age or the age of the spirit. More important than that, we showed them that we understood that the army is a young person's profession, and to be leaders in it, we have to stay young physically and in spirit.

On Thanksgiving Day, a couple of young soldiers came to my house for dinner. They had also played two football games. They were in some obvious discomfort, but didn't try to hide it—like I did. One thing I couldn't hide was my stiff neck. I believe I got that from watching youngsters run by me going the other way while I was making desperate pawing grabs for their flags.

My wife was able to put these two young soldiers into food comas fairly quickly. I was in one too, but I wasn't going to show my pain. Around halftime of the Redskins and Cowboys game, the youngsters were coming out of their comas and making their way to the dessert tray—again.

While I was holding my belly and praying for a burp, my wife reminded me that I needed to act my age when I was eating or I'd be sorry later. Replying with one of those macho, guttural grunts, I moved out to the dessert tray and secured some more pumpkin pie—two scoops of Cool Whip, please. I was sorry later, but not much.

The day after Thanksgiving, my belly was still hurting from eating, and my body was aching from playing football. Thinking of the youngsters, I told myself I'd bet they were hurting too. I thought about acting my age. I didn't know what that meant. A lot of folks sharing my biological age don't play sports anymore (unless golf counts); they don't occasionally pig out, and they don't secretly tap their toes to rock and roll. But I do. Because soldiers are young and "their hearts are touched with fire." All of them. They expect that of their leaders, too. When I'm not like that anymore, I'll move on to walks in the park and stuff like that.

Drill Sergeants

Drill sergeants are the hardest-working soldiers in the army. They wrote the definition of tough love. Our army's success is directly tied to the job done by these professionals and dedicated trainers.

The closest term in the dictionary is *drillmaster.* A drillmaster, according to the dictionary, is an instructor of military drill who maintains severe discipline and often stresses the trivial.

If you ask a private in basic training what a drill sergeant is, the definition will be based on what has happened in the last several minutes. Ask a spouse, and the answer is likely to be "not home." Ask another sergeant, and the answer will probably be "crazy." Ask a drill sergeant, and if he or she has time to be bothered with you, the answer may be:

"I am a teacher, trainer, father, mother, brother, sister, chaplain, and hotel manager; I am hated, loved, envied, respected, clean, and shiny, and I never sweat. I am up at three A.M. so that I can be cleaned and shined in time to be at work at four to do the paperwork before five when the day starts. I am loudly running soldiers out of the dining facility at seven P.M. in the hope that I can finish the day's counseling by nine, be home by ten, and in bed by eleven when the day ends.

"I know my children as lumps in a bed. They are there when I leave and there when I get home. I am a perfectionist and have a difficult time settling for less. I refuse to accept being second-best because the business I teach gives no prizes for second. If I were standing in the middle of ten fat, sloppy sergeants, someone would notice a scuff mark on my boot. I dislike parents and recruiters in general because of the raw material they send me, but I know why I'm here. I know my job better than anyone does. Just ask me.

"I love what I'm doing, but complain about it constantly to my peers. I never complain to anyone else. In fact, I only socialize with drill sergeants. I can give you a purpose for everything I do. I am many different things to many different people. I know I am the first example of a noncommissioned officer soldiers ever see and the one they will always remember. I do stress discipline, but I am never trivial."

Bilko or Rambo

This is a topic I've been known to sermonize on to great lengths sometimes. I'll spare you that, but it's an important and often overlooked aspect of our business. Giving it some critical thought may give you that added urgency you need when considering the importance of the example you provide soldiers to follow.

Remember that noncommissioned officers must set the example we want soldiers to follow. Because of that, it's critical to understand what must be overcome to develop trained and disciplined soldiers.

Each year since our army became a volunteer force, the number of military veterans has decreased. The many base closures produced by our force reduction are also limiting our contact with civilian communities. Because of that, the average child growing up today will have limited contact with soldiers.

Their expectations of what a sergeant is may be based on the portrayals brought to them in the cinema with surround sound. They may expect us to be bumbling idiots, con artists like Bilko, Rambo-like one-man killing machines, or a Jack Daniels–guzzling collection of drug-crazed killers. On the other hand, they may expect the less-than-flattering real-life images of a couple of sergeants at Aberdeen Proving Ground.

The example we set and the role models we must be to

overcome those possible perceptions become even more critical as our army grows smaller and its contact with the civilian community lessens. When a youngster from the street meets a real sergeant, it must always be reinforced to that youngster that no one is more professional. We do that by living the values and challenging soldiers to use us as their standard and model, and by constantly reinforcing— by walking the talk—that we're neither Bilko nor Rambo. Simple enough?

Summary

- Leaders must always be conscious that wherever they are and whatever they are doing, they are the role models soldiers will try to copy. Their most important role-modeling task is fulfilling their soldier care responsibilities.
- Units become the mirror image of their leaders. As a leader, you must be aware of your sphere of influence—your three-meter zone—and use it as your mirror for your own self-assessment.
- Everyone has expectations. We must try hard to live up to soldiers' expectations of us as leaders, and we must make our expectations of other leaders our standards for performance.
- Leaders must give credit to the led when missions are successfully completed.
- We are in a young person's business. We must show soldiers by our example of fitness and our willingness to engage them on that level that we understand that.

- One of the most important things we must know, while setting the proper example for soldiers, is the image of noncommissioned officers they may bring with them to the army.

CHAPTER FOUR
COMMUNICATING

Noncommissioned officers must be able to express ideas effectively, both orally and in writing.

Noncommissioned Officers Can Write—and Should

Nor can a sergeant or corporal be said to be qualified who does not write and read in a tolerable manner. —*Baron Frederick Wilhelm von Steuben*

A necessary tool for noncommissioned officers (NCOs) is the ability to express their thoughts in writing. NCOs have to plan, prepare, and conduct training; counsel and communicate instructions to subordinates; work through problems; and make well-thought-out decisions. The ability to frame their thoughts in writing is critical to all those processes. Developing and communicating a leadership philosophy, for example, is impossible without the necessary writing skills.

I can't lay claim to being gifted with any special talent for writing, but I work hard to express my thoughts in a simple and straightforward manner. I'm not a writer in a journalistic sense, but I do write a lot, because writing is an important thinking tool for me. Expressing my thoughts in written form causes me to think them through more carefully than I would otherwise. I have often sat down to write my thoughts on a subject and watched my position change right before my eyes.

Putting your thoughts on paper causes you to see things that you previously overlooked. Writing is where we do our best thinking, I am sure. When our ideas are in front of us to see, they represent what others will hear when we express our ideas to them. It gives us the opportunity to question whether what we have to say makes sense. It also gives us the chance, for example, to see if what we have to say is going to offend anyone. (Maybe offending someone is our intention. If so, we have the opportunity to refine that thought, like any other, before expressing it.)

It's time for a "when I was a first sergeant" story. I was the first sergeant of a unit in which it wasn't always easy to get the principal NCOs together on short notice to discuss issues. When I needed to let them know something or to share my thoughts on an issue that couldn't wait until my weekly NCO call, I would write out what I wanted to say in memo form and send it to them.

One young sergeant, who thought highly of himself and worked in the headquarters, didn't particularly care for my technique, mostly because he was consistently guilty of the activities of which my memos were consistently critical. The sergeant shared my memos, and I'm sure his opinion of them, with the command sergeant major. (Both of these NCOs had very short, negative stints in my three-meter zone.)

The command sergeant major called me into his office to discuss my method of communicating thoughts to the NCOs of the unit. He told me that he didn't think I was a very good writer and that either I didn't know the army's writing program very well or I chose to completely ignore it. If I was writing this stuff, he said, he didn't know when I had time to be a first sergeant.

I thanked him for his critical opinion of my writing skills. Then I told him that I thought communicating with the NCOs in the unit was a major part of my job. I asked him whether there was something else he had called me in for, or whether he had forgotten to put the bottom line up front. My attempt to show my knowledge of the army's writing program was not very amusing to him. He got a little red-faced and launched into a tirade of gutter lingo that's not worthy of committing to print. He told me not to write any more of my cute little memos (the bottom line he failed to put up front). "Cute" wasn't exactly the descriptive four-letter word he used, however. He chose another word, which ended with "-ing."

When he said he didn't have anything else for me, I left. I never stopped writing the memos. After that, I cranked one out every chance I got. One of my favorites was about three-meter sergeants and their poor performance at physical training. I wrote it at just about the same time that the command sergeant major failed his physical fitness test and got to retire for his effort. Odd how things work out sometimes, isn't it?

Getting back to the point, writing is a necessary and important skill for noncommissioned officers. There are two things you need to do to improve your skills if they need it. Read a lot and write a lot. It doesn't matter what you read. Spending your time wisely and doing professional reading is best, I'm told. Nothing, however, can replace the stress relief and escape gained from reading well-written fiction. You can get the best of both worlds by reading historical novels such as *The Killer Angels*.

If you are working on a project or have ideas or thoughts, write them out. Write out your thoughts the way you would want to speak them. You'll find that your verbal skills will improve, too. The more you write, the easier it gets and the better you get at it. If nothing else works, try keeping a daily journal. Write down your thoughts at the end of each day. It's a small investment of time that will develop an invaluable tool for you.

One more war story, and then I'll move on to something else. As a member of the Enlisted Special Review Board, my job, like that of the other members, was to research and write board opinions on evaluation report appeal cases. We were also asked by the proponent to recommend changes to the regulation governing enlisted evaluations if we thought changes were needed.

One change we strongly recommended was that the enlisted system have a referral process like the one in the officers' system. The officers' system lets the rated officer write what amounts to a rebuttal for an adverse report. The rebuttal gets filed in the officer's official file with the report. The retired officer in charge of that operation said he couldn't support our recommendation. He said most NCOs couldn't write well enough and would do themselves more harm than good.

There are many boneheads who think like that. I expressed that thought to him very eloquently, too, I might add. The reason folks think that way is that NCOs do not write enough. It has nothing to do with their ability. NCOs can write, and should.

Today's Buzz Phrase Is . . .

The chief merit of language is clarity, and we know that nothing detracts so much from this as do unfamiliar terms. —*Galen*

Noncommissioned officers—all leaders, actually—communicate more orally than in writing. We have to communicate our thoughts clearly and in a form that is easily understood. We must always be conscious of the effect our words have on others.

Sometimes an important leader coins a phrase or uses a quote from history, with good intentions, that takes on a whole new meaning by the time it gets down to soldiers. "Can-do attitude" translates into "get the job done at any cost." It ranks right up there with "make it happen." "Second to none" produces "zero defects." We get so wrapped up in buzz phrases that we sometimes toss them out there as solutions to problems. Doing that puts our subordinates in the predicament of trying to live up to an empty buzz phrase. Soldiers will "make it happen" if that's the instruction they get with no latitude to investigate a different way. They will not disappoint you. They may break several other things along the way, but the "it" you asked for will happen.

> Effective communication occurs when others understand exactly what you are trying to tell them.
> —Field Manual 22-100, *1990*

When you communicate instructions to soldiers, be careful that whatever you communicate is clear. Soldiers will do exactly what you tell them to do. That point was constantly stressed to us in drill sergeant school. It proved to be sound advice when dealing with new soldiers. It's good advice for dealing with seasoned soldiers, too.

I remember one of my drill and ceremonies tests in drill sergeant school—aligning the squad. After giving the command to the squad to dress right, dress, I moved to my position by the squad leader to check the squad's alignment. I then instructed the number-three man to move up two inches. The number-three man, another student, shot a fleeting glance at the instructor and then jumped up into the air a couple of inches.

The rules we followed in school required us to do exactly as we were instructed or get nailed for failure to follow instructions. (Getting nailed in drill sergeant school for failure to follow instructions during drill and ceremonies usually meant you got to repro-duce the section of the field manual you had broken in three original handwritten copies.) It created a lot of comical situations for us, but it made the point to be clear when giving instructions to soldiers—because soldiers, in their zeal to please you, will do exactly what you tell them to.

Sadly enough, I've seen soldier problems discounted with buzz phrases. It's one of the most serious problems born of rhetoric and buzz phrases. Still, we all know that "when the going gets tough, the tough get going."

A blow with a word strikes deeper than a blow with a sword. —*Robert Browning*

Soldiers become what you tell them they are. Sometimes we communicate with soldiers and never consider the effect our words may be having on them. This is a problem. Drill sergeants have their own favorite names for soldiers. I had mine, too. I used to call them boneheads. It was my way of telling them I was not exactly pleased with their performance at a particular time.

I've gotten smarter in my old age. I know, for example, that people will become what you tell them they are. I've seen it too often. Children repeatedly called stupid by their parents believe they are and act accordingly. Soldiers constantly called boneheads by their sergeants will come to believe they are boneheads. The problem is, they come to expect nothing more of themselves than a bonehead performance, and that's what they give you. Soldiers become what you tell them they are, and they achieve what you tell them they can achieve.

Your message should be easy to understand, serve the purpose, and be appropriate for your audience. —Field Manual 22-100, *1990*

I'll make just one more point on oral communication with soldiers. Know to whom you are talking. When I worked on the special review board, the personnel command (PERSCOM) command sergeant major gathered up all the sergeants major he could and had us go to the barracks at Fort Myer, where the PERSCOM soldiers lived. He got us in the unit's day room and started talking. He pulled out his wallet and took out a card. He held out the card and asked, "How many of you remember how to set the headspace and timing on a .50-caliber machine gun?"

This was a room full of mostly adjutant general corps (AG) sergeants major. The command sergeant major was an infantryman. His point was lost on a room full of soldiers who probably had been on the same installation with a .50-caliber machine gun but never close to one. Surely they knew nothing about setting the headspace and timing on one.

The command sergeant major was trying to make the point that you forget things if you don't do them once in a while. In this case, he wanted to stress that we needed to know how our soldiers lived in the barracks, and the only way we could do that was to visit the barracks once in a while—just as he would revisit the training aid he carried in his wallet when he needed to remember how to set the headspace and timing on a .50-caliber machine gun. Another expression more familiar to a collection of AG soldiers would have better made the command sergeant major's point.

Talk to people in real words that have substance and meaning, and not in empty buzz phrases. Remember to be clear in giving instructions, because soldiers will do exactly what you tell them to. And finally, know to whom you are talking, and talk to them in terms with which they are familiar.

Thompson's Rules

I try not to mention individuals by name when writing down my thoughts. Someday, this stuff may be found in an old footlocker, and some good friend of mine could be embarrassed, or some other good friend might feel left out because I didn't mention him or her. Well, for the sake of this discussion, I have to break that long-held rule.

Colonel Gerald Thompson was the commander of the 26th Support Group during some of my time as a first sergeant there. He was the commander when it was a deployable unit, before it became an area support group. Colonel Thompson was a friend to soldiers and was always genuinely concerned about them. But that's not the only thing that keeps the colonel in my memory and that made him a charter member of my personal three-meter zone. Just as important was his ability to bring folks back to reality and get them to use their God-given common sense when approaching soldier business. He did this with what I call Thompson's Rules.

The first time I ever heard one of the rules was in a discussion about some landscaping and grass that had footpaths in it, where folks took the most direct route to get where they were going instead of using the geometrically laid-out sidewalks. If the landscape designers had used Thompson's rule for sidewalks, they wouldn't have had that problem. Thompson's rule for sidewalks says: "Plant the grass this year; next year, come back and put a sidewalk where the path is." I can show you sidewalks in Patrick Henry Village, in Heidelberg, Germany, that follow that rule. They were constructed during his watch.

Once, during a quarterly training briefing, a company commander kept getting himself into trouble. The commander's training plan wasn't bad, but his presentation of it was. The captain was working hard to impress the colonel with his training knowledge and briefing skills. One wrong response to an inquiry by the colonel would lead to another question and another wrong response. That was the first time I heard Thompson's rule of holes, when he explained it to the young captain: "When you find yourself in one, son, quit digging."

The colonel taught me some valuable lessons with his rules. The wit of his rules was not the lesson to learn. The lessons amounted to these two things: Simplify all things and apply good common sense to them; and the right expression communicated at the right time is an effective tool to bring folks back to reality. These are lessons all of us can learn and apply to our lives and our jobs in the army.

You can probably think of many examples where the application of some of Thompson's Rules could have made a difference in your unit or the lives of your soldiers. We owe it to our soldiers and the army to apply common sense to what we do, and to use it to examine what others want us to do as well.

We also have to communicate that to our bosses from time to time, because they too can slip. Remind them of Thompson's rule for sidewalks. It's a rule that has a way of bringing folks back to reality and causing them to use common sense before spending resources. Keep in mind that resources also include people. The commonsense approach may cause them to not have to refer to Thompson's rule of holes.

Summary

- Written and oral communication skills are critical to leading. We must work hard at both to ensure that we can communicate our thoughts and instructions to soldiers. Writing skills require effort to maintain, but are a valuable tool for leaders.
- Leaders must be aware of the impact of verbal communication and the harm that can be done. Verbal communication must be clear and easily understood.
- Well-chosen words, communicated at the right time, are effective tools for bringing folks back to reality and causing them to apply common sense

PART TWO: THE SOLDIERS

Soldiers coming into the army expect their leadership to provide training and direction, provide discipline, administer justice fairly and equitably, set a
moral and ethical example, give counseling and career guidance, and be a font of knowledge and experience from which to draw. If we, as the leaders
in the army, don't do this, we are failing the soldier
and the army. —Department of the Army Pamphlet
600-65, *November 1, 1985, attributed to Sergeant Major
Vallair*

CHAPTER FIVE
STANDARDS AND DISCIPLINE

Noncommissioned officers must know, abide by, and enforce standards.We must be models of self-discipline while insisting that appropriate discipline is used in developing soldiers.

Standards

A disorderly mob is no more an army than a heap of building materials is a house. —Socrates

Did you ever hear the expression "the industry standard"? That means that if you are in the business of providing a product for consumers, it must meet a certain standard to be acceptable. It means that everyone in the business agrees on what a widget is supposed to look like, act like, and do. Then, when someone says, "I need a widget," that person knows what to expect, and we all know what "widget" means. This ensures that no one skimps on a standard, providing the public with a shoddy product that doesn't get the job done.

Soldiers also serve the public. The product we provide is their defense, safety, and peace of mind. We have established standards for our product, too. We have developed them over a period of some 200 years. We have standards for things as seemingly insignificant as how we dress and as complicated as how to maintain the most advanced main battle tank in the world. Meeting seemingly insignificant standards is as important as meeting the most complicated ones—meeting one establishes the foundation for meeting the other.

> You owe it to your men to require standards which are for their benefit even though they may not be popular at the moment. —*Gen. Bruce Clarke*

Standards start with noncommissioned officers (NCOs). A soldier wanting to know the standard is not going to look it up in a book. A soldier will use a noncommissioned officer as the standard. Soldiers will meet the standards set by and follow the examples of the NCOs in their three-meter zones.

Standards can be made too hard or too easy when people add their own criteria to them. Noncommissioned officers can't allow that to happen.

Everyone has heard of the physical training test no one could pass. I had two soldiers returned from a primary leadership development course for failing the physical fitness test. It turned out that both had been graded by the same NCO at the school. A check with the school showed that the NCO had failed 16 of the 20 soldiers he graded on the test that day.

I questioned the failure of these soldiers because they had both had above-average test scores only days before going to the school. The school commandant was adamant that the grader was right, although we learned after checking that he was the only grader who had such a high failure rate for this one test. Was he too hard, or were the other graders too easy? I think you can draw your own conclusion.

Standards are not arbitrary. They are established over time. Noncommissioned officers cannot add personal twists to standards, making them too hard or too easy. Standards have to be consistent so that soldiers know what to expect. A standard in one part of the world today must be no different from a standard in another part of the world tomorrow. We have to avoid creating a "standard of the day" environment.

Discipline

Discipline, like standards, starts with noncommissioned officers. Discipline comes from self-discipline. Self-discipline is simply making yourself do what you know has to be done without anyone looking over your shoulder and reminding you to do it.

It is easy to skip physical training on a morning after a night when you didn't have much sleep or when the weather is not ideal. It's easy to cut corners during recovery after a field exercise when everyone wants to go home. A leader who does either of these things shows a lack of self-discipline. No one stands over leaders' shoulders and tells them how to act in these situations. The decisions leaders make are indicators of their work ethic and their level of self-discipline.

If a leader delays complete recovery of organizational

equipment for personal reasons, the message sent to soldiers is that it must be OK to delay recovery. That display of a lack of self-discipline causes soldiers to not do full recovery on individual equipment. It teaches soldiers that it's OK to put other things ahead of the mission. It lays the foundation for not doing what everyone knows needs to be done. It teaches bad self-discipline habits. Bad self-discipline turns into poor discipline overall, leading to poor unit discipline. There are many, many rules and regulations in our everyday lives, by which we are expected to abide. No one stands over us constantly to make sure we do as we should.

Discipline starts with good self-discipline. A well-disciplined unit comes from soldiers with good self-discipline, learned from following the example of noncommissioned officers displaying good self-discipline habits.

Discipline practices, like standards, need to be consistent. Soldiers have to know what to expect from their leaders.

People make honest mistakes. Soldiers are people. A mistake made during an honest effort to get the job done normally doesn't require disciplinary action. It's better corrected with leadership, teaching, and counseling. A good leader turns those mistakes into positive learning experiences. Of course, tolerance for those types of mistakes decreases as the rank and experience level of the person making them increase.

Disciplinary action is required for any intentional violation of rules or regulations. It must be swift and suit the infraction. That point is just not negotiable.

How do you know if a lapse of discipline—a "mistake"—was intentional?

The short answer is that you have to know the soldier. Soldiers know what must be done. When you are convinced a soldier knew what had to be done and the standard by which to do it, and still didn't do it, you have a lapse of discipline, not a mistake.

What if a new soldier makes the "mistake"—a soldier you don't know yet?

Look at the severity of the mistake, and look at the circumstances. Was it a minor error in judgment, or was it a blatant act of being undisciplined? That is a decision you will find relatively easy to make once you thoroughly examine the situation. Of course, depending on the severity of the act, the benefit of the doubt should go to the soldier. A real three-meter soldier will make another "mistake" and won't be very long about it.

When it comes to discipline, we spend a lot of time considering what's too hard and what's too easy. "Too hard or too easy?" is not the question to solve when dealing with discipline issues. It's a matter of the right way and the wrong way to deal with them. The corrective action taken must suit the infraction. The goal of corrective action is teaching the soldier the right way.

A soldier who fails to prepare his or her individual equipment for inspection is a discipline issue. A soldier who is caught in possession of illegal drugs is also a discipline issue. Do you handle both the same way? Of course not. A soldier who does not prepare for inspection when told, unless it's an old habit, is better dealt with through corrective training that teaches the necessity of equipment readiness. The soldier in possession of drugs has committed a crime and should be dealt with accordingly.

Noncommissioned officers usually find themselves in the position of advising commanders on the degree of punishment to administer when it's required. This is one of the most important roles played by NCOs. There are some serious considerations to make when recommending punishments. Remember that commanders are men and women just like the rest of us. They take no great joy in punishing others. Their human reaction is to want to share that unenviable task with others. That sharing comes in the form of seeking your advice.

When advising a commander, there are some things you ought to think about. Never sign up for message sending. I have had commanders tell me, more than once, that I have to send a message to the rest of the unit that this behavior will not be tolerated. This kind of thinking often leads to a degree of punishment that is harsher than warranted. The most important point to make to the commander is that the act of taking disciplinary action sends the message, not the degree of punishment administered.

The other thing the NCO must do is to make sure the commander has considered all aspects of the case before administering punishment. Sometimes that means you have to become an advocate for a soldier whom you know is wrong and deserves to be punished.

I had a case once where a staff sergeant, only months from a twenty-year retirement, was charged with driving while intoxicated (DWI). The commander was adamant that he wanted to reduce this staff sergeant one pay grade. His argument was, "I've reduced everyone who has come before me in DWI cases; what kind of message will this send?"

I explained to the commander what the actual cost to this NCO would be if he was reduced. The commander had not considered that a reduction would mean a considerable loss in retirement pay. The effect would be a fine the NCO would be paying for the rest of his life. In this case, the commander reduced the staff sergeant anyway.

The message he sent was not the message he wanted to send. DWIs in the command were not significantly reduced, and every leader started recommending more lenient punishments across the board. It was like the thought process some folks attach to award recommendations. "I will recommend a higher one because that is what it takes to get the lower one I actually want." In this case, subordinate commanders and NCOs started recommending punishments below what they actually felt were needed. The commander could no longer tell if a recommendation for leniency was real or not, because of the message he had sent to the leadership.

Soldiers learn the importance of standards and discipline from noncommissioned officers. Soldiers will attach as much importance and significance to them as their closest NCO leaders do.

How do you convince soldiers that following rules through self-discipline and adhering to standards is the only acceptable way to do business?

One of the most important leaders in my three-meter zone, my dad, rest his soul, told me a story once that he said had been told to him by my grandfather. It was during one of those frequent conversations we had in which I either had failed to do something I was supposed to do or had done something I should have known better than to do. I have always remembered the story and its point. It still applies, and it answers the question.

"We had an old mule when I was a boy," my dad told me. "My dad used him for just about everything. He would use him to drag logs out of the woods, pull up stumps, or pull the plow when it was time to plow. Whenever he was working this old mule and he passed by our apple tree, the mule would stop working and start eating apples. My dad would take out an axe handle he kept handy, walk around, and bust this old mule right between the eyes with it. What he did was to convince the mule that work produced a much more pleasant outcome than stopping to eat apples."

I got it, Dad.

I don't recommend busting a soldier between the eyes with an axe handle, and I doubt that my granddad hit that mule, either. The point made with the illustration is: Make sure you convince soldiers that following rules and meeting standards produces a much more pleasant and positive outcome than getting sidetracked by something else.

Where Do You Draw the Line, Sergeant?

I've often heard that the difference between an army and a mob is discipline. Because of that, we have to do things correctly in the army. The result of doing what's right is important. It also has a more lasting effect than just accomplishing the mission at hand.

In the army, for any topic you choose, there is usually a clearly defined right way to deal with it—a standard. Some soldiers are not always focused on doing things right. They are not focused because they have a confused definition of "right." To them, "right" equals what's convenient, what they like, or what is to their advantage at the time. But in fact, the right way has nothing to do with our personal preference, convenience, or advantage. What's right is our published standards, rules, and laws, and what we know to be legal, proper, and moral.

Noncommissioned officers are the army's standard bearers. Because of that, we have to insist that soldiers do things the right way—legally and to the standard. In drill sergeant school, we were taught to "insist and assist." NCOs have to insist that standards be met and assist soldiers with meeting them. When we wear the noncommissioned officer rank, we are mandated to insist that standards are met and rules are followed. We assist soldiers by training them to standards and giving them candid reminders when they are failing to measure up. Insisting that things be done right causes soldiers to direct their efforts toward what's right. It has a positive influence on their lives and our profession. Soldiers live and are developed in the environment created for them by their leadership.

> Our troops are capable of the best discipline. If they lack it, leadership is faulty. —*Gen. Dwight Eisenhower*

NCOs are obligated to create a positive environment in which things are done right and standards are enforced. In such an environment, soldiers, prone to wander back and forth across the line between what's right and wrong, accept that there is a right way and pursue it instead of pursuing a convenient, easy, or advantageous way. They develop positive habits.

Don't get the impression that doing things right is uncommon in our army, because it isn't. However, attempts to do things other than the right things happen often enough to deserve comment.

How often have you seen soldiers bolt for the door during reveille or retreat? One morning, while out running, I was right beside the flagpole when reveille sounded. Coming to a dead stop is not the way I like to end a run, but in this case, it was the right thing to do. So I did it.

While I was standing there, saluting the flag on its way up the pole, I caught a glimpse of some soldiers running toward an open doorway. I also saw a few soldiers, who I imagined might be waiting for their morning formation, slink down into the seats of their parked vehicles. I even saw some vehicles drive by, with the drivers pretending that they didn't know what was going on.

When you are only a few meters from a flagpole, with a cannon with smoke coming out of it and loudspeakers blaring music, and when the majority of the people are saluting, there is very little chance that you don't know what's going on. I confronted all of the soldiers I could catch up with. When questioned, they all admitted that they knew the right thing to do. The question to resolve is why they didn't do it.

Most mornings, I jog through intersections where the traffic flow is supposed to be controlled by stop signs. At o'dark hundred in the morning, I found out it's routine for folks to ignore those signs with little hesitation, especially when they think no one is looking. It makes me want to go check the signs and see if maybe somewhere in fine print under "STOP" they say, "only if someone is looking," or "optional." If you are the only person around, you are still obligated to follow the rules and live up to your own standards.

A staff sergeant walked by me once with his trousers bloused wrong. They were wrapped and pegged tightly around his leg. I asked him if he knew the right way to blouse his trousers in accordance with the uniform regulation. He responded that he did. He also explained, with a little insistence from me, what the right way was. Of course, I pressed the issue by asking him, if he knew the right way, why he didn't do it that way. His reluctant response was a mumbled, "I don't know, Sergeant Major."

The "why" answer in these examples, and many similar ones you can probably think of, is no mystery. The answer is a lack of self-discipline and self-control shown by these soldiers. These undesirable character traits are usually a product of the environment created for the soldiers by their leadership. It's an environment in which some leaders are reluctant to take corrective actions when necessary. It's also an environment in which leaders set a bad example by themselves showing a lack of self-discipline. In our profession, corrective action is always necessary, and self-discipline is critical.

By now, you are probably thinking that the examples I gave are minor and questioning what harm was actually caused. If our self-discipline is such that we can't obey the simplest rules that we write for ourselves, then there is cause for concern. According to the leadership doctrine we have written for ourselves in *Field Manual 22-100*, self-discipline is "forcing yourself to do your duty—what you ought to do." In this case, what we ought to do is live within our own rules and standards and insist that everyone else does.

> Perhaps the most valuable result of all education is the ability to make yourself do the thing you have to do, when it ought to be done, whether you like it or not. This is the first lesson to be learned.
> —*Thomas Huxley*

Doing what we like or prefer instead of what we know to be right is potentially serious. There are no varying degrees of seriousness when it comes to doing what's right, especially when you factor in the possibility of lives being lost. If we knowingly choose to disobey rules and regulations and disregard standards, even if they appear minor, we have to consider what the full ramifications of our choices are. As leaders we have shown soldiers, who look to us for the proper example, that it must be OK to disobey some regulations sometimes.

Tomorrow, when those soldiers are noncommissioned officers, they may choose to look the other way when a soldier is not meeting some other standard that they consider insignificant. They may count an extra hit to allow a soldier to qualify with a weapon. If we are only talking about one hit, what's the harm? If we demonstrate to soldiers that it is acceptable to overlook some standards, or some rules, we are asking for all rules and standards to be questioned. Worse yet, we are training our replacements to act in this manner.

Most of us know the right things to do, and we do them. Along with that, we have to use a couple of those Cs we hear so much about: candor and courage. It's easier and more natural to just let something go than it is to look a stranger in the eye and tell that person when he or she is not meeting a standard. We have to have the courage to tell soldiers, point-blank, when they are not meeting a standard or doing what's right.

Then we are obligated to define "right" for them. We define "right" with well-known and published rules and standards. We do not define "right" with an opinion. Certainly, there are some rules and policies with which we disagree. Disagreeing, in the proper forum, is something we are allowed to do. Disobeying or disregarding is not something we are allowed to do in any forum. If we selectively obey regulations written with the best interest of the entire group in mind, where do we stop?

A gym bag that is worn over the shoulder while in uniform. A hairstyle that is a little too faddish. Trousers that are pegged. Pass rules that are interpreted to suit the occasion. Soldiers running from flag call. Fudging on an established standard. Headgear worn on the back of the head with bangs hanging out the front. All of these minor violations of standards add up to a lack of self-discipline and knowledge of the standards by soldiers. Letting all of these violations go uncorrected shows a lack of courage and candor on the part of the leadership. Can it get any worse than that? I don't know. Where do you draw the line, Sergeant?

Summary

- Because of standards and discipline, our army has survived. The NCO role is that of the standard bearer for the army. Not only must NCOs know and live the standard; they must also enforce it.
- An NCO must be able to distinguish between honest mistakes and acts of being undisciplined. NCOs must be models of self-discipline and consistently enforce all standards.
- Even seemingly insignificant rules and standards are important because they establish the foundation for following the more difficult ones.

CHAPTER SIX
KNOW THEM

The greatest leader in the world could never win a campaign unless he understood the men he had to lead. —*Gen. Omar Bradley*

The Three-Meter Zone

There is no one best leadership style. What works in one situation may not work in another. . . . You must develop the judgment to choose the style that best meets the situation and the needs of the subordinate. —Field Manual 22-100, *1990*

There is no one style of leading that suits every occasion or every leader. There is a solemn truth about leading, however. All leadership is important, and the most critical leadership takes place in the three-meter zone. Picking a leadership style is a lot like getting dressed. What you put on has to fit you and be comfortable. It has to be something you are proud to wear in public. It has to fit the occasion.

I'm sure you've all read *Field Manual 22-100, Military Leadership.* And if I picked any one of you and asked you to tell me about it, you would give me a list of factors and principles and everything a leader must be, know, and do, right out of the manual. And that is all great information. The problem I have with it sometimes is that it's too much information for me to sort out and use when I need it. To make it work for me, I had to simplify it. Let me give you my simplified version and tell you what I think it takes to lead and understand the soldiers you are trying to lead.

First of all, if you want to be consistent as a leader, you need rules to go by. I picked two rules that work for me. My first rule is something we all do every minute of every day. Consciously or not, we lead by example. The second rule is to never forget what rule number one is.

In addition to rules, leaders need priorities to give them direction. My priorities are high standards, a high state of discipline, self-discipline, a high state of soldier and equipment readiness, professional development for noncommissioned officers (NCOs), and leaders who are positive role models. In "Leaders' Priorities" (Chapter 2), I told you where those came from.

To go along with those rules and priorities, you need a leadership style or technique to use. *Field Manual 22-100* gives you three: directing, participating, and delegating. But choosing a leadership style is not as simple as knowing what those are and just picking one. You have to consider a number of things before you select a style. Mostly, you have to know the soldier you are leading.

I call my technique for selecting a style the three-meter zone. It works like this. I believe there are three types of soldiers. I call them three-meter, fifty-meter, and 100-meter soldiers. Each type requires a different leadership style. We will talk about each one in detail. You can categorize soldiers in your mind any way that works for you, but three, fifty, and 100 meters is a context I can understand. It helps me to know with whom I'm dealing and helps me pick the style I need to use.

When I went through basic training, a lot of emphasis was placed on mines and booby traps used in Vietnam because they were causing many of our casualties. I remember a demonstration that had to do with an antipersonnel mine called a Bouncing Betty. When stepped on, this mine bounces up about waist-high before it detonates. When it detonates, as you might expect, the results can be devastating.

The instructor told us that if you are within three meters of this weapon when it detonates, you probably will not survive. At fifty meters, he said, your chances for survival improve dramatically. At 100 meters, you are relatively safe from this weapon. After listening to that instructor and seeing pictures of intestines hanging out, I was sure I never wanted to be caught in the Bouncing Betty's three-meter zone. Leaders also have a three-meter zone.

Three-meter soldiers need constant attention. If they don't get it, they will do something that causes you to give them some attention. They'll get busted for driving while intoxicated (DWI). They'll beat up their spouses. They'll take drugs. They'll write bad checks. They'll forget to come to work. Or, when they do finally come to work, they will have appointments, most of which will continue to extend their temporary "no physical training" medical profiles.

You can't give these soldiers the attention they need unless you keep them in your three-meter zone. When you give them missions, give them detailed instructions. Make sure you tell them who, what, where, when, why, and how. Then tell them all the negative things that will happen if they fail to complete the mission. Keep reminding them of the dangers of being in your three-meter zone.

You never have to highlight the positive to three-meter soldiers, because they fully expect to receive impact awards for any missions they complete, even if someone else completes the missions for them. You have to constantly check on three-meter soldiers and remind them of their missions, because they lose track of what they are supposed to be doing. On the other hand, if you lose track of them, they will wander out of your three-meter zone.

The problem with that is that they usually wind up in the first sergeant's three-meter zone. This, of course, means you have to go into the first sergeant's three-meter zone to get them back. If you spend too much time in the first sergeant's three-meter zone, he or she will start to question your maximum effective range.

By design, life in the three-meter zone is extremely unpleasant. Life expectancy in the three-meter zone is very, very short. In fact, no one survives the three-meter zone. Because in the three-meter zone, the intensity of the fragmentation when a leader detonates is too much for three-meter soldiers to survive. Your job, though, is to help them survive.

A leader must suppress the bad and bring out the good in each soldier. —Field Manual 22-100, *1983*

The only way they can survive is if you get these soldiers out of the three-meter zone. To do that, you give them two survival options.

First, you tell them what actions they must take to get out of your three-meter zone. You have to make it clear that all of their negative attention-getting activities have to stop. No more DWIs. No more spouse beatings. No more bad checks. Then you tell them what the standards are and what your expectations of them are. You tell them to concentrate on what all soldiers need to concentrate on: accomplishing their duties to the utmost of their abilities. You tell them that if they do these things, they will get out of the three-meter zone and be headed for the relative safety of the fifty-meter zone.

When three-meter soldiers respond to the first option, immediately reinforce the positive. Make sure they understand that you and others do recognize and appreciate it when they do the right things.

If three-meter soldiers don't respond to their first survival option by taking the actions laid out for them, you have to resort to a second option, one which meets your obligation to the army and to the other soldiers: ending their careers as soldiers, and doing it as fast as possible. Whichever option they take, the end result must be the same: that they leave your three-meter zone.

Next are fifty-meter soldiers. Some soldiers start out in the fifty-meter zone, and some go there from the three-meter or 100-meter zones. No matter how they get to be fifty-meter soldiers, they require the fifty-meter leadership style.

I just told you how three-meter soldiers get to the fifty-meter zone; 100–meter soldiers usually get there because of some negative experience. It could be anything from a soured marriage to not being selected for promotion. This is a tough time for these soldiers. With the right kind of leadership and positive encouragement, you will get them back to the 100-meter zone. Without that leadership and encouragement, they could be headed to the three-meter zone.

When you give fifty-meter soldiers a mission, you need to give detailed instructions. You finish up your instructions by telling them the positive things that will come from successfully completing the mission. Fifty-meter soldiers are looking for positive things to happen in their lives. Their desire to have something good happen and their willingness to work for it are what move them to the 100-meter zone.

Once you've given a mission to fifty-meter soldiers, you need to check on them from time to time, because they might need a little direction or redirection or a pat on the back. They need to know that you are interested in whether they successfully complete the mission. Remember, when they do complete the mission, they expect something positive to happen. That positive action can be as little as a pat on the back and some kind words, but it needs to be something. Your goal is to move these soldiers out to the 100-meter zone, where the survival rate is high.

One hundred–meter soldiers are what we want in the army. One hundred–meter soldiers are grown by positive leadership that teaches them how to do their jobs while constantly reinforcing the positive habits required to be an effective leader or soldier. When you give 100-meter soldiers a mission, all you need to do is tell them the desired result, provide them with a timeline and the necessary resources, and point them in the right direction.

You can be confident that they are going to get the job done, because the way they were brought up constantly reinforced the importance of getting the job done. They know, without being told, that positive things come from getting the job done. They also know, without being told, about the three-meter zone. All these soldiers need from you is a glance in their direction once in a while, just to let them know that you know they are there and that you care about the job they are doing. One hundred–meter soldiers are not driven by the fear of the negative or by the possibility of reward. They are driven by the satisfaction of successfully completing the mission.

There you have it. *Field Manual 22-100* simplified: two solid rules, some priorities, and a technique for selecting a leadership style.

Welfare Soldiers

We used to say you could count on them to show up for work on payday. With direct deposit, you can't even count on that anymore. As one of my NCO heroes put it, "They're using up air that good soldiers could be breathing." Somewhere after thieves, liars, and drug addicts, they're about the worst brand of three-meter soldiers you'll ever encounter: welfare soldiers. They fall just below wet toilet paper on the usefulness scale. They're everywhere in the army, and if you're reading this, you know some of them. These soldiers are not typical three-meter soldiers, who usually need only focus, direction, and insistence to become better. They are a disgrace to the profession of arms and a detriment to readiness.

The leadership environment creates welfare soldiers. Just like good soldiers, welfare soldiers grow to be what they are. Their behavior is learned from and reinforced by poor leadership and poor leadership practices. It's leadership that lets them survive the three-meter zone.

Make sure you can identify them when you find them. Here are some of their characteristics: They demand all the benefits and services that come with being soldiers—they are first in line for everything good and first in line to complain if they don't get it. Work, permanent change-of-station moves, deployments, training, and any other soldierly obligations are very low priorities, because they interfere with their personal lives and personal time. The idea of selfless service is lost on this group. Welfare soldiers and the leaders who create them are a blight on our army that we need to ferret out and get rid of. Sound strong? Well, I hope to heck it does.

Welfare soldiers use up many resources. What's worse is that good soldiers have to do what they fail to do and go where they fail to go. Their excuses to get out of soldierly obligations are endless and often incredible. This is especially true when they are faced with leaving comfortable garrison jobs for line units, or with the possibility of spending time as field soldiers or on deployment.

Many of their excuses are downright funny, but they're also a detriment to the readiness of the army and the morale of good soldiers. Welfare soldiers don't shoulder their share of the burden—or any other part of it, for that matter. While they pile up excuses, other soldiers deploy and spend Christmas alone in mud holes like Bosnia and deathtraps like Somalia. Many good soldiers and their families move all over the world while welfare soldiers play the system for their own benefit. Good soldiers carry the load while they sit in easy assignments, holding down part-time jobs and finishing college degrees.

These soldiers expect the army to adapt to their personal needs and make exceptions for them at the expense of other soldiers and readiness. No corporation could make such concessions and survive. The army, especially today's overdeployed and underresourced army, can't either. If these soldiers were not in the army, we'd find them on street corners with signs reading, "I'm homeless, need help, God bless you," and they would be drawing welfare checks. American taxpayers get no return on their investment from this group.

When welfare soldiers are not trying to get out of assignments and work, you can find them sitting in a doctor's office. Their goal: tailor-made medical profiles that keep them from doing anything physical except sitting and breathing—at their own pace.

What's really disgusting about this whole business is that when good leaders hold welfare soldiers to standards, they very quickly discover that we have some welfare leaders, too.

A welfare leader creates an environment in which welfare soldiers grow and prosper. These leaders do not have the courage to look welfare soldiers in the eye and tell them they don't measure up. Instead of challenging them for failing to meet obligations, they let it go. It becomes easier and easier for them to send other soldiers on assignment in a welfare troop's place, especially when the other soldiers are faceless and do not offer up a cargo pocket full of excuses for not meeting obligations.

Real leaders, however, face an onslaught of questions about the actions they take to make welfare soldiers do what's right. The welfare soldiers' mastery and use of the complaint system bring about this onslaught. It's a complaint system obviously designed by a welfare leader. Forests full of trees die answering the inquiries generated by the complaints of welfare soldiers.

In the meantime, the complaint system does what it appears to be designed to do. It creates delays long enough for welfare soldiers to be deleted from assignment instructions, or whatever their goal is, so they can start the process all over again. The best situation for welfare soldiers is when good leadership rotates out so they can run their games again on new leadership. Their fallback, welfare leaders, always seem to be there when they need them.

For the benefit of the soldiers who successfully move through the three-meter zone, draw the line on welfare soldiers. They, too, must move out of the three-meter zone. Once you've accomplished that, you can tackle those welfare leaders.

Tweeners

Do you know what a tweener is? A tweener is a person whose God-given attributes place him or her somewhere between great and pitiful. Tweeners fall in between great commanders and poor ones, great NCOs and poor ones, great leaders and poor ones, and great soldiers and poor ones.

They're also somewhere between genius and idiot, fat and skinny, athlete and klutz, fast and slow, short and tall, handsome and ugly, humorous and depressing, rich and poor, powerful and weak, tactful and rude, religious and atheist, leading and following, in touch and out of touch, happy and sad, liberal and conservative, loud and quiet, profane and holy, considerate and thoughtless, generous and stingy, moral and immoral, ethical and unethical, happy and sad, concerned and unconcerned, egotistical and modest, humble and arrogant, kind and mean, literate and illiterate, slick and rough, shrewd and dull, devious and forthright, winner and loser.

Most soldiers are tweeners. When we accept that, we are better people and soldiers. We also learn that tweeners are not so bad.

First Impressions

First impressions are usually erroneous and . . . every man will become better or worse. —Department of the Army Pamphlet 22-1, *1948*

You only get one chance at a first impression, they say, and it's hard to overcome a bad one. We've been implanting that thought in our minds and teaching it to soldiers for as long as I can remember. Just as the old field manual states, it's a rare first impression that pans out. It's important to look and act professional all the time, not just the first time. It's even more important to get beneath the shiny or not-so-shiny surface when forming a professional opinion of a soldier.

> Rash Judgments. This is the tendency to evaluate a soldier on the basis of appearance or of a specific behavior trait. For example, some people will say of a neatly dressed soldier passing by, "There goes a good soldier!" —Field Manual 22-101, *1985*

In the army, at least during my time in it, most leaders have been guilty of a bad habit. We make judgments about soldiers based first on how they look. Once we have gotten past their looks, we start stereotyping them by their specialties. You know: clerks and jerks, spoons, tread heads, legs, grunts, and so forth. Add to that all the other preconceived notions and stereotypes of people we've been carrying around as baggage for years, and it's a wonder we can make accurate assessments of anybody, especially after one look.

Making a judgment about someone based on how they look is probably the best argument that can be made for throwing away anything resembling an official photograph. I knew a fat guy in Korea who was rumored to have had his head put on a photograph of a not-so-fat body and sent it off as his official photograph. I'm not sure I ever believed it, but he did get selected for promotion by that particular sergeant first class board. He certainly would have been a lot prettier if there had been less of him to look at.

I've known folks to look at a soldier's official file and form their entire opinion of the soldier based on the height and weight notations in the record, often not considering that the file also contained an excellent performance record, including frequent mentions of high fitness test scores, excellent fitness habits, and the fact that the soldier had been the same size throughout a successful career.

> Stereotyping. This involves judging soldiers on presumed group physical or behavior characteristics. Examples include the false judgment that all big soldiers are slow, all thin soldiers are weak, or all soldiers with high foreheads are intelligent. These notions are seldom correct. Evaluations should be made only on a soldier's demonstrated behavior or on his demonstrated ability.
> —Field Manual 22-101, *1985*

We have been conditioned over time to believe that heavy equals lazy, slow, and probably not too smart. If a person is short as well as heavy, we think that he or she is also insecure. Then, God forbid, if that person turns out to be something other than white, male, and Protestant, we've opened a whole new can of worms. That's how shallow thinkers and those who do no thinking at all make judgments about the abilities of people.

Sadly enough, we use the same approach to formally evaluate soldiers. Right on the Noncommissioned Officer's Evaluation Report, there is a bullet that asks us to rate a person on whether that person looks like a soldier.

Well, that would be fine, but what exactly does a soldier look like? No one has ever taken the time to explain that one to me. Are they tall, short, skinny, fat? What? I do know that when we see a pretty one, or one that ain't so pretty, we often make invalid assumptions about that person's ability to soldier based on appearance. We make these assumptions before we check to see if the soldier knows his or her business. We do that because of that first impression. Be cautious in your first assessment of soldiers. It could be fatal.

Nelson and Pineapple

If you've been in any unit in the army, you know Nelson and Pineapple. We had them both in my basic training company, and I've had them both in every unit I've been in since.

Nelson was not a bad soldier in terms of discipline, but he managed to stay in trouble with the drill sergeants anyway. He never learned how to make a bed, shine boots, get out of the barracks on time, put his field equipment together, do his laundry, or get anything completed on time. He would always miss a spot when shaving, have his trousers partially unbloused with boot strings hanging out, and have his pockets unbuttoned. One of Nelson's platoon mates was always there to fix Nelson or whatever Nelson broke.

None of us knew Nelson very well, but we made him the brunt of our jokes. We never knew him because no one ever took the time to sit down and talk with him. We would see him sitting alone in the mess hall and in the barracks, and he would stay to himself during breaks. I guess you stay to yourself if the only communication you can look forward to from your platoon mates is some kind of wisecrack.

Pineapple was a big strapping kid from Hawaii, nicknamed by the drill sergeants. Pineapple was physically strong. He would often finish a road march with a couple of his platoon mates in tow. He was popular with his buddies and was always the center of attention. I suppose we all thought he looked like a soldier, too.

Almost daily, wherever we were on Fort Ord, we could hear the coughing, "hrrump, hrrump, hrrump" sounds coming from the hand grenade range. To a trainee, there is no other sound quite like it.

"Tomorrow, you'll be on the grenade range, men," our drill sergeant told us. "It's the one place in basic training where you can die if you don't pay attention." He used to give us these kinds of talks sitting in the platoon area. It's when drill sergeants take their hats off and sit down and talk to you. When no other drill sergeants are around, they don't posture or try to impress anyone with how tough they are.

He was dead serious this time and wanted us to be a little bit afraid, I think. He told us a story every trainee has heard. It was about the trainee who released the spoon on the grenade and then regrasped it, thinking he'd made it safe again. A few seconds later it blew his head off and killed the instructor with him. He wanted us to be thinking about that the next day, and we were.

Like every training day on a range, this one started with a safety briefing. The sergeant told us how important it was to pay attention to the instructions we were given and obey exactly all commands given by instructors. We were told not to touch anything we might see lying around on the range if we could not positively identify it. We were shown different types of hand grenades, training grenade fuses, and other things. We were told that if we saw any of this stuff where it shouldn't be, we were to notify a drill sergeant or instructor right away. It was demonstrated for us how much damage a training grenade fuse could cause. An instructor pulled the pin on one and set a C-ration meal box over it. It blew the box apart. Everyone went to great lengths to stress the potential dangers of the day's training.

We sat in the bleachers for the beginning of our training. We learned all about the different types of hand grenades and their uses. With his explanation, the instructor would demonstrate them for us. I remember how vividly purple the purple smoke grenade was and how brilliant the thermite grenade was as it burned its way into an engine block. Finally, we got around to learning about fragmentation grenades.

The instructor put a lot of emphasis on the damage a grenade could inflict on a person. He showed us different types of grenades, pointing out the coloration and markings so we would know when we had the real thing.

The instructor told us we would throw two real ones after we finished training, practice, and the qualification course. Then he asked for a volunteer. Of course everyone in the platoon offered up Nelson as the volunteer, so Nelson it was.

The instructor called Nelson down in front of the bleachers. He told Nelson he was going to have him throw a hand grenade, but since Nelson hadn't been through the hands-on training yet, he wasn't allowed to pull the pin. The instructor showed Nelson how to stand, how to hold the grenade, and the right way to throw it once the pin was pulled. He asked Nelson if he understood, and Nelson nodded.

He positioned Nelson just where he wanted him and brought out an ammunition box. He carefully removed a grenade from the box, brought it over, and placed it in Nelson's hands without letting go of it. He reminded Nelson and us that Nelson wasn't trained, so the instructor would have to pull the pin before Nelson could throw the grenade.

The instructor asked Nelson if he was ready, and Nelson nodded again. The instructor began to carefully pull the pin from the grenade, and then, suddenly, lying on the ground in front of the bleachers was a grenade with no pin in it. The instructor yelled, "Live grenade!" and ran for cover.

While most of us in the bleachers froze like deer caught in headlights, Nelson calmly bent over, picked up the grenade, threw it over the wall, and got in a prone position as he had been instructed. A couple of seconds later, while most of us were about to pee in our pants, we heard the firecracker pop of a training grenade fuse. The instructor came out and told us that had that been a live grenade, Nelson would have saved our lives, because he didn't panic and remembered what he had been taught. We all had a different opinion of old Nelson after that.

After a day of throwing practice grenades and going through the qualification course, we finally got our opportunity to throw live grenades. I can't recall the number of three-sided concrete bays we had to throw from that day, but because of a significant emotional event, I recall almost everything else.

When I finally got into a bay with a drill sergeant, I saw that his campaign hat had been replaced with a red steel pot. The sergeant in the range tower talked us through all the commands, and we pretended to throw a couple of times. He wanted to make sure we knew what to do at each step, how to get down after throwing, and what to do in case of an emergency. Frankly, I was a little nervous. A few more practice throws would have been just fine with me.

The drill sergeants gave us our live grenades when instructed to by the tower. We took the grenades in our throwing hands as we had been instructed. We held the spoons down with our thumbs if we were right-handed and with our other fingers if we were left-handed. In the ready position, we each put the thumb of our other hand under the safety clip and our forefinger through the pull ring attached to the safety pin. The drill sergeant never took his eyes from the grenade once he placed it in my hands.

The tower NCO asked the drill sergeants if they were ready on the right and left. They indicated that they were by raising their hands. The next command was, "Twist pull pin, prepare to throw!" That was our command to pull the pin from the grenade and assume a throwing position with our nonthrowing hand pointing toward our target and the grenade cocked behind our ear. I did that and assumed that everyone else did too. Suddenly there came a set of frantic commands from the tower: "Throw, throw, throw!"

As it turned out, old rock-solid Pineapple had thrown his grenade while the rest of us were standing there in our perfect throwing positions, preparing to throw. Pineapple was getting into a safe prone position while we were all standing exposed and watching his grenade bounce downrange. He didn't throw it very far, either, for a big guy.

Everything kind of went into slow motion after that. I actually remember wondering how much of Pineapple's three- to five-second fuse had ticked away while the rest of us were standing there exposed. I came back to reality quickly when the drill sergeant yelled, "Throw, damn it, throw!" I did, and was being assisted to the ground when I heard the "hrrump!" from Pineapple's grenade, followed a couple of seconds later by the others. Needless to say, we all had a different opinion of old Pineapple after that

Get Beneath the Surface

More often than not, the first judgment made of a soldier is based on appearance. A judgment is made about physical fitness, professionalism, competence, and everything else. Leaders need to get beneath the surface when forming their opinions of soldiers. When we get beneath the surface, we find out what an individual is really about.

I was fortunate one day to have a conversation with a retired sergeant major of the army. The sergeant major of the army complimented a soldier who worked for me on how good he looked. He then said that he could remember when it was easy to look at a soldier and tell what the soldier's specialty was. He said mechanics looked like mechanics, clerks looked like clerks, and cooks looked like cooks. "Nowadays," he said, "you have all kinds of soldiers looking as sharp as this one, and you can't tell anything about them by looking at them."

We are all guilty at one time or another of making bonehead judgments and categorizing soldiers because of their appearance. How many times have you stumbled upon a soldier wearing every conceivable qualification badge and looking like he or she might have just fallen off a recruiting poster? Your first impression was probably that you had a "hooah" superstar on your hands. How often have you found out later that hooah was a mile wide, but only an inch deep? Sometimes these superstars spend so much time trying to get scare badges on their uniforms that they fail to learn how to do their jobs along the way. Hooah?

We have to get past this first impression test in the army. We have to pick up our soldiers, shake off all the glitter and dust, and get beneath the surface. Only then will we know if a cook can cook and if an infantryman really is one. Be wary of first impressions.

Stay Focused—Stay in Touch

I know my soldiers and I will always place their needs above my own. —*The NCO Creed*

It is easy enough to provide soldiers with their basic needs—food and shelter, for example—but it takes skillful, imaginative, and dedicated leaders to create

an atmosphere where soldiers and their family members share a sense of purpose and belonging.
—*Gen. Maxwell R. Thurman*

A noncommissioned officer's focus must be on soldiers and their needs. We stay focused by determining how all issues affect our soldiers. While keeping our focus, we need to avoid some pitfalls. We need to avoid weighing the value of a program based on its impact on us personally, or charging into it with emotion and personal bias. Neither allows intelligent examination of an issue's impact on everyone.

A program may not be the best option for us personally. Rarely is a program the best for everyone. That doesn't mean it isn't the best choice for the greatest number of soldiers. We are obligated to look at things that way for our soldiers. Officers, looking to us for experienced soldiers' perspectives, need us to examine issues that way as well.

As NCOs, our focus is on soldiers' needs, not the budget or the bottom line. Determining soldiers' needs is important. We approach it with the same concern and urgency with which we approach developing a unit's mission-essential task list.

Mission-essential tasks are just that—essential. Accomplishing them is critical to a unit's success. The availability of resources is not considered when developing mission-essential tasks. Determining needs cannot be resource-driven either. The fact that we might not be able to pay for something doesn't make it any less of a need, just as a task is no less essential because of a lack of resources.

Meeting soldiers' needs is an unwritten essential task for an organization. Determining soldiers' needs and making them known to the command is an essential task for all NCOs. It's the command that must decide whether and how to apply resources to meet them. Remember that meeting the needs of soldiers may be dependent on resources. Determining them never is.

Meeting soldiers' needs is critical to supporting unit missions and the mission of the army. Organizations sometimes forget that.

During one of my tours in Germany, we had a recurring problem with getting the gymnasium open at 6:00 A.M. to support unit physical training programs. On discussing it with the gymnasium staff, I was told that it was not their mission to open early in the morning three days a week to support unit physical fitness programs. You can picture the twisted expression on my face at hearing that response. Their mission, they said, was to provide support to the community for recreation and unit-level sports programs. The budget (isn't it funny how the budget or the computer takes a beating when something is broken) would not allow them enough hours to open early three days a week.

What they really told me was that they were not willing to adjust operations to meet the needs of soldiers. That caused me, as it should any NCO, to question whether they were focused on what it is we do.

Service providers in military communities must always return to one unchanging fact when deciding how their services will be delivered to soldiers. The job of soldiers is to fight our nation's wars, or to engage in operations against hostile forces in support of our nation's political objectives. Noncommissioned officers are obligated to make sure service-providing organizations keep that focus. It's in our creed.

In this case, the service provider, the gym, lost that focus. If it were focused, providing services to ensure that our soldiers got what they needed to meet the mission, which included physical fitness training, would not have been a question. The question would have been, "What recreation and sports programs can we afford to keep?" Supporting soldiers' physical fitness, a need, should never have been a question.

To keep everyone focused on soldiers' needs, non-commissioned officers have to stay in touch with what those needs are. With the best intentions of meeting soldiers' needs, we sometimes fail because we let ourselves get out of touch with what their needs really are.

Before we go on, let's discuss the difference between a want and a need. I have often heard from senior, influential, and intelligent people the following: "That is something [the soldiers] want; it's not something they need. Our job is to meet their needs."

I'm sure you agree that food, clothing, and shelter are needs—obvious needs that we unquestionably meet. We have to dig deeper than that, though, because all needs are not so obvious.

There are many things leaders routinely write off as wants that are real needs for soldiers. Is privacy a want or a need? There are times when a person needs to be alone. Privacy, the ability to get away from it all, is a human need. That makes it a soldier need. Privacy where soldiers live, for example, is a need. Think about the first thing you notice when you walk into a room shared by two soldiers. You notice the barricade they have constructed so they can each have a private corner.

Too often, we don't view privacy as a need for our soldiers because it isn't one for us. We go home at night. We leave the job behind. We get away from the people we work with every day. Our need for privacy is met. Some of our soldiers live and work in the same building. Mentally, they never get away. The mission does not always allow for privacy. When it does, we have to see that the need is met.

When we first looked into putting hamburgers in field rations, the response was predictable. Young soldiers thought it was great. A lot of old soldiers said, "Soldiers don't need that stuff; why are we wasting time with that?" I remember old soldiers saying the same thing when I was a private and the army started letting mess halls have short-order lines for lunch.

These same old soldiers get very passionate about such issues and expend a tremendous amount of time and energy trying to stop them for no practical reason. Amazing, isn't it? Especially considering that our young soldiers throw away more of their field rations than they eat. A hamburger is a more appealing meal to these soldiers than chicken à la king. Of course, if it's fortified with all those things a soldier needs, we both win. The soldier's and the army's needs are met.

We get out of touch in other ways that cause us to not meet the needs of our soldiers. One of those ways is getting caught in a time warp. A time warp is when your mind stays in 1968 and your body moves on out to 1998. You may have this problem if you catch yourself humming the Rolling Stones tune "Time Is on My Side" or some other song from your past.

> Leaders . . . must not be tied inflexibly to policies of the past that may not apply to fast-moving situations of the present. —*Maj. Gen. Perry Smith*

I knew a first sergeant who really devoted his time to improving the place where soldiers lived. He had day rooms that were carpeted and paneled. They had nice furniture, magazine racks, and television sets. They were beautiful—just what he had wished he had when he was a private living in the barracks.

His soldiers, however, never went into those beautiful day rooms. Why, you ask? It's simple. Those day rooms did not meet the needs of the soldiers of the day. The soldiers of twenty-five years ago would have loved those day rooms, because that was exactly what they wanted in their day rooms—twenty-five years ago, when the first sergeant was a private. The first sergeant's soldiers, though, wanted arcade video games, satellite television, and a place where they could have social gatherings and listen to music together, not just a quiet room where they could sit and watch TV or read.

If the first sergeant had just looked around or asked the soldiers, he would have known what was needed for those day rooms to be used. He had good intentions, just out of touch; he didn't know his soldiers. He was meeting the needs of soldiers when he was a private; he was doing it that way because when he was a private, his needs were not met. I know because I was that first sergeant. Don't get caught humming an old tune.

To end this discussion, let me try to make it clear. If a soldier wants something to the point where it affects morale, it also affects performance. That's when a want becomes a real need. It's a part of our charter as an NCO corps to know soldiers, stay focused on them, and stay in touch with their needs.

Culture Clashes

> I was moving among two groups . . . who had almost ceased to communicate at all, who in intellectual, moral, and psychological climate had so little in common that . . . one might have crossed the ocean.
> —*C. P. Snow*

Knowing soldiers and what they need also involves knowing where they came from. After we've been in this business for a while, we sometimes forget that. An NCO must know and understand the environment that produced the raw material he must turn into soldiers and the influence it had on them. NCOs have to always think about that and try to understand it before they can deal with it.

We know that the values held by many new soldiers are not compatible with the army's values and culture for any number of reasons. We have to keep in mind that:

- They may have grown up in an environment that does not emphasize the value of human life.

- Extreme acts of violence may have been common-
  place where they grew up. At a minimum, they
  have been bombarded with violence on the television news and in the movies and may have come
  to accept that as the way life is.
- They may have experienced open use of and dealing in illegal drugs, other criminal activity, and
  many other lifestyles not acceptable in the army.
- Based on their exposure to many things, they may
  have a very contorted image about what a soldier
  is and does.

We counter those influences by ensuring that soldiers
are taught from the beginning about values, responsibility, and the dignity and worth of individuals. We have to
teach them the importance of teamwork and placing the
needs of the group ahead of their personal desires, a difficult task when many of them may have been fending for
themselves for quite some time.

We can't fix what's broken in the culture outside our
gates, and it's not in our charter to try. But we do have to
understand the significant influence it has had and may
continue to have on our soldiers and the difficulties we
face when weaning them from it.

Noncommissioned officers must shape the values and
character of soldiers, because they are our replacements.
We can do that successfully only if we teach them that soldiers and units survive because of intangibles such as values, a sense of purpose, discipline, self-discipline, obey-
ing laws and rules, and caring for each other.

Knowing your soldiers means that you know what must

constantly be stressed to develop their character. Knowing them starts long before they show up in a reception station.

Which Came First—the Problem or the Stress?

Stress is the body's response to a demand placed on it. The demand may be physical (cold, injury, disease) or mental (fear, conflict, pressure).
—Field Manual 22-100, *1990*

I can't remember the first time I heard about the S word. Like many others, though, I finally had an explanation for all my ails. Whatever the shortcoming, stress did it. If I didn't have something going on at the moment, then the post-traumatic version of the feared S word was the root of all my problems.

How often, recently, have you heard the blame for a really serious crime placed on a supposed post-traumatic stress reaction to something that happened forty years ago? A female politician was tried for contracting a hitman to kill her husband and her lawyer. They captured her on tape recordings sounding very much in control. Her defense was that she was not in control of her actions because she was sexually abused as a child, more than forty years earlier. She had committed no other known criminal acts in her life and had no other episodes of not being in control.

How long before we hear this? "Forty years ago my dad cuffed me alongside the head after I walked the length of his brand-new Hudson with a big nail I'd found lying in the yard. That post-traumatic stress reaction is why I beat my child into a pulp today." Or, "My mom and dad were married for forty-nine years. They yelled at each other once in a while. My repressed memories of those episodes are why I threw my wife through the window, Your Honor." If the Nazi war criminals had only been aware of that defense, what would have happened? Post-traumatic stress reaction instead of "I was just following orders." Right.

I'm not a cynical person. At least I don't think so. Sometimes, though, I believe all the highfalutin excuses we come up with for our behavior are just that: excuses. When we, using all of our God-given wisdom and several Ph.D.s, can't explain why someone did something dumb, we say stress must have done it. We scoot right over the problems, it seems, and hang everything on stress.

Why else, do you think, would a postal worker return to his former place of employment and start shooting his ex-bosses and ex-coworkers? Was it because he was a pitiful employee who was deservedly fired and sought to take a little revenge? Nope. He was a drug-addicted Vietnam veteran unable to overcome the baby-killer image heaped on him by a collection of ungrateful, unbathed, scraggly social rejects calling themselves the American conscience, back in 1968.

Or was it because of all the combat he saw in the Saigon bars (because, you see, he was a clerk who never saw any combat except for pictures in the *Stars & Stripes*) twenty-five years ago, so that he is now suffering from post-traumatic stress syndrome? I buy that. Don't you? I will, just as soon as you can explain to me why there are many, many Vietnam veterans who were knee-deep in a lot of bad situations and who are not shooting up the damn post office!

I have my favorites, too. Take the drug-addicted professional millionaire, the twenty-year-old athlete who can't handle the overwhelming stress of playing a game at a level equal to his salary, so he turns to cocaine, loose women, and the wild life. Or his salary doesn't quite come up to his Deion-esque self-evaluation, a.k.a., ego. I am now supposed to share his stress and long to join him in group hugs. Because, oddly enough, he turned up HIV-positive or just checked in to the Betty Ford Center. OK!

So, really, what exactly is stress? Can you point to something concrete and say, "There it is; that's stress"? Stress is one of those things, I'm told, that is locked away inside your head. It's how you react to situations, both positively and negatively. A 300-pound defensive end bearing down on a quarterback is not stress. The quarterback's reaction to the defensive end is stress. He either stays calm and with his protection or panics and later regains consciousness while looking out the ear hole of his helmet.

Did you see the movie *Apollo 13*? If I had to put a picture of stress in the dictionary, that would be one I'd consider—that or the image of nineteen-year-old kids hunkered down behind their sandbags at Khe San. Or I'd use a picture of an American soldier standing in the food stamp line. Those are pictures of stress.

Nowadays, though, we too quickly paint a stress picture to excuse just about anything. Ask a soldier why he or she did something dumb. For instance, "Why did you drive your car past the commanding general's house, the wrong way down a one-way street, with your 1,000-watt stereo shaking the house's foundation, while registering a blood alcohol content of 2.0?"

Today's answer is very likely to be, "Well, I was just stressed out, man." Unfortunately, when you ask the same soldier why he or she shook a newborn baby until its innards turned into Jell-O, you're likely to get the same response. Stress did it.

I'm certainly not trying to make light of what is a real problem for some folks. I fear, though, that we are letting stress become an excuse for behavior. Instead of looking for real causes for problems, we are lumping everything under the S word. Let's get to work on what caused the stress and fix that. If it's stress we are working on, we're too damn late.

Compare two soldiers. One is working continuous twelve- to fourteen-hour shifts, separated from his family in a foreign country, the danger of death or serious injury always present, and the living conditions deplorable. This soldier is constantly alert and constantly thinking of survival, and there is no reprieve from the environment. No real rest. No relaxation. Nothing.

The other is financially strapped because all the credit cards available are maxed out. Most of the paycheck is used just to meet the minimum payments. There is a DWI charge pending. The spouse has said, "I've had it." Regular duty is interfering with the part-time job, making those credit card payments even tougher. On top of all that, there is the absolute horror of facing the devastating two minutes of push-ups, two minutes of sit-ups, and a few minutes of running.

Who has the stress here? Oh, they both do. The issues

for NCO leaders, however, are, "At what point should these soldiers have gotten my attention?" and, "Could I have predicted or even prevented the stress problems if I had known them better?"

One situation is all self-inflicted. If I am going to call myself a leader, I had better know the difference and be prepared to deal with each appropriately, and at the right time. I just have to know which came first—the problem or the stress.

Inspector Generals

The inspector general (IG) is an important asset for leaders. The IG is an organization's honest broker and can have a very positive effect. If the IG is not cautious and doesn't do the right things, however, he or she can have a very negative impact on soldiers and leaders in the three-meter zone. You have to know your IG.

In my early days in the army, units went through annual IG inspections. Looking back, I don't think it was a very effective inspection program. We would spend a week or two doing the paperwork we were supposed to have done during the past year. If there were extra parts in the motor pool or supplies in the supply room, they went into the back of somebody's car.

The first sergeant had one duty roster for the IG to look at and another one he really used. Everybody knew that. The one he really used went into the back of the car along with the rest of the stuff he had in his cardboard box, such as his slush fund. Top also sent the unit's boneheads away on detail somewhere. Just like the stuff in the cardboard box, they needed to be out of sight when the IG came around.

We would spend a week working nights—cleaning, painting, cutting grass, raking, and adding some eyewash wherever the first sergeant could find a need for it. The rest of the time we would spend working on personal equipment for the inspection. On inspection day, there would be an in-ranks inspection; the barracks and our gear would get the once-over; the IG would look through the unit's files (constructed just for the occasion); and then the IG would be gone.

After that, the first sergeant would form the unit, and the commander would tell us what a great job we had done. The boneheads would come back from wherever Top had sent them, all the boxes would come back out of the cars, and we would forget about those useless forms and reports until the next IG inspection—the next year. Every IG inspection team knew those things happened. After all, they hadn't always been IGs.

We never heard much about anybody complaining to the IG in those days. I went to the IG once as a young soldier. It wasn't my idea. It was the first sergeant's, and he took me. I hadn't received any pay for three months. Top got the IG involved, and my pay got fixed. I never heard about anyone taking trivial complaints to the IG; maybe it happened, but I didn't know of it. That was my early experience with the inspector general—a positive one, in which the chain of command turned to the IG when problems couldn't be resolved. It was a positive experience because the leadership knew their IG.

I was fortunate to be a first sergeant for four years. During those four years, I was blessed with great IGs. I guarantee their greatness didn't stem from always seeing my point of view on issues. They were great because I could always pick up the phone and get their help, making sure I wasn't about to do something dumb.

They were always willing to spend time to help me be a better first sergeant. More often than not, they would come to me and tell me about potential problems and make recommendations on actions to take to preclude them. They were proactive, knew what was going on in the command, and created a positive work environment. Because of their approach to business, I never felt I was in an adversarial relationship with an IG. They made a significant contribution toward making my time as a first sergeant a positive, successful leadership experience.

When I got to one army command, however, things were different. There, I met my first three-meter IG. He spent a lot of time entertaining frivolous complaints from soldiers with incredibly poor performance records and histories of discipline problems. The relationship his office maintained with leadership was adversarial. The office had a reputation for putting together inquiries that drew conclusions based on one-sided, partial information. The common expression among leaders was that the IG's system for handling complaints was receive complaint, draw conclusion, prove conclusion. Leaders did not trust this IG to provide fair, unbiased information for them to use.

It was common knowledge that inside this IG's offices, command sergeants major were referred to as the CSM Mafia, even by the IG himself. That's like referring to a group of people with a racial slur. It plants a bias in the minds of those doing the investigating. When that happens, they don't investigate complaints; they investigate a member of the Mafia. It also created an environment in which the leadership quickly moved to nonjudicial punishment when they could have given soldiers another chance.

Leaders in the command didn't feel they had the kind of IG relationship I had come to know during my time elsewhere in the army. Picking up the phone and asking for advice or an opinion just wasn't done. The fear was that a question would generate a silly inquiry—on you. It was a bad environment, which rendered the IG useless to the command and even more so to the group who needed him most—NCO leaders.

When an IG creates this type of environment, it creates a lot of pressure on leaders. There are a couple of lessons here for NCOs to counter that pressure. The first one, obviously, is to know which of your soldiers are prone to trotting off to the IG with problems before they bring those problems to you.

Some go because they are hoping for the IG to hammer the leadership that has probably held them to unpleasant standards. Some are malcontents and make a career of IG visits. They spend more time in the IG's office than the IG does.

Sometimes, however, they go because they have real problems that leadership has failed to deal with. The first leadership failure in this case always happens in the three-meter zone—the zone that surrounds the soldier and his or her first-level NCO leader. Go there first when trying to figure out why a soldier went to the IG and not to the chain of command for problem resolution. React to problems, not IGs, and don't wait for the IG to construct his or her version of what happened.

Next lesson: Know your IG, and make sure your IG knows you. Face it; some IGs attract complaints because of how they react to them. An IG who constantly reacts to frivolous complaints will obviously attract more complaints. Don't beat up the complainer in cases like this; beat up the IG. Don't develop an adversarial relationship, but make sure this person understands that just because he or she is the IG, it doesn't mean he or she is always right. These IGs rarely if ever reconstruct an accurate picture. What they have to offer is an opinion; you have one too.

This kind of IG needs your help. There is rarely an occasion when someone doesn't know a malcontent is on the way to the IG. Pick up the phone and give the IG your version of the issue first. Relieve that pressure by letting the IG react to you. It works.

Don't Worry, They'll Fit

Well, CG, I'm sitting here stimulating the right side of my brain by listening to Beethoven. In September 1971, I was going through the central issue facility at Fort Ord, California, getting my initial issue of uniforms when I met my first Department of the Army civilian. He was an older gentleman. By the time I got to his spot, I was wearing fatigue trousers, a T-shirt, and low-quarter shoes, and dragging a duffel bag that held everything else I had been issued thus far.

Looking up from my clothing record, he peered over his bifocals at me. "What size, son?" he asked me. To which he got the "I'm a confused trainee and I don't have any idea" look. He looked me up and down for a moment, then tossed me a couple of poplin shirts from off the shelf and said, "Try these." There was a little more room in the chest and neck of these shirts than I thought I needed. "Don't worry, son, in two months they'll fit." And then he yelled out, "Next." You know what? After two months, they fit just fine.

I've met a lot of army civilians like this gentleman. Many have been in the same jobs for a long time and know them very well. If they tell me something will fit, more often than not it does. I hear a lot of soldiers say stuff like, "That old civilian has been doing the same job forever." When I hear that, I tell them they have been doing the same job for a long time too. The difference is that they haven't been doing it in the same place.

Army civilians are no different from soldiers in most respects. They come from different backgrounds, cultures, religions, genders, and value systems. Some are dedicated professionals who dearly love being around soldiers and giving them support. Some of them are where they are for reasons only they know. And, just like soldiers, some work for the army and some work for a paycheck.

Civilians, unlike soldiers, didn't sign up for physical training and combat skills. Some soldiers and some civilians realize what those differences entail and accept them. Some don't. There certainly are periodic culture clashes that can be solved with interaction and education. Let me explain.

A sergeant first class came to me once with a poorly written evaluation report. "Poorly" is probably an understatement, but it's the only adjective I can think of right now. He came to me to complain about the report, wanting me to call someone we'll call Mr. Smith, give him a hard time, and tell him to rewrite the report. I told him I would certainly do that as soon as he explained to me what he had done to make sure Mr. Smith understood the enlisted evaluation system.

Mr. Smith, it turned out, had never rated an NCO and knew nothing about the system. To him, it was just a matter of filling out a form, and he thought he had done a fine job of it. With a little bit of education about the system and the importance of the report, Mr. Smith did a good job the next time. I have rated civilians using their system. I was just as lost and confused as Mr. Smith was, until someone—a civilian—took the time to explain the system to me.

When I was a first sergeant, some soldiers complained to me that their civilian supervisor would not let them participate in physical fitness training because they came to work too late on physical training days. I learned two things in my conversation with this civilian supervisor. First of all, he was not aware that it was a regulatory requirement for soldiers to be given physical fitness training during on-duty time. What I didn't know, however, was that these soldiers were coming to work at 9:30 A.M. on physical training days instead of 8:30 A.M. like all the other soldiers in the unit.

NCOs and many civilians assume that the other knows things while having no basis on which to make that assumption. Let me try to simplify that. If a civilian turned up in your sector in a combat zone, would you assume the civilian had the necessary skills to survive? Would you toss the civilian a protective mask and say, "Put this on if we get gassed?" No, you'd show this person how. Have you made any assumptions lately?

I don't know if any civilians, other than the one I know about, will ever read this. But if any do, you need to understand some things about soldiers and NCOs, too. If you are in a job in which you handle the same types of problems for soldiers frequently, they have probably become routine for you, and you are probably very good at solving them.

Understand that these problems likely aren't routine for each soldier. The urgency they feel about getting their problems solved may bubble over into frustration if they don't detect some urgency or compassion on your part in solving the problems. Some of us shoot off our mouths when we feel those frustrations, but remember, it's the problem, not you, that frustrates us.

Soldiers do not understand eight-hour workdays. They always show up on your doorstep five minutes before quitting time with a problem they believe needs to be solved now. Never say, "We're closed; come back tomorrow." Take a few minutes to hear the soldier's problem, and he or she will understand when you explain why you won't be able to fix it until the next day. The soldiers won't understand if you don't take the time to listen. This is a lesson many NCOs need to learn, too.

Remember that no matter how far removed from soldiers you may think you are, whatever you do has some impact on them. Never take that lightly. If you are in a decision-making position, get a soldier's perspective on an issue before you make a decision that affects them. Please do not get that perspective from your civilian coworker who retired from the army twenty years ago, because soldiers and the army both have changed. Things will be different now.

For NCOs, I offer this. Civilians have pay problems just like soldiers do. They have personal problems and families; they get sick and need time off once in a while, just like soldiers do. If they work for you, they need your guidance, mentoring, understanding, and counseling, just like soldiers. If you work for them, they deserve your support, loyalty, and the same advice you would give to any superior on issues that directly impact soldiers.

You will find army civilians wherever you go. Even when you think you are on the most remote deployment known to anyone, an army civilian is going to turn up there sooner or later. I'm having a difficult time finding a difference here, if you haven't noticed. But maybe that's the point I've been trying to make all along.

Army civilians and soldiers enjoy good relationships when they make an effort to understand and accept that each has a different role to fulfill. When you put them together in an organization doing a job, make sure you develop that understanding, and then "don't worry, they'll fit."

How did I do, CG?

(By the way, CG is short for Change Guru. This is the nickname I gave Ms. Carolyn Smith from the Fort Myer Office of Change Management, who encouraged me to keep plugging away at this book and to add this section on army civilians.)

Summary

- Before a leader can lead effectively, he or she must know whom he or she is leading. Different soldiers require different leadership styles. Those requiring the most leading and personal attention are usually found in the leader's three-meter zone.
- Some soldiers do not get better. They insist on staying in your three-meter zone and avoiding soldierly obligations. You need to move them out of the three-meter zone.
- Most soldiers, like most leaders, are just average people. The sooner we accept that realization, the better off we'll be.
- Assessments made of soldiers based on first impressions are rarely accurate. Assess individuals based on their demonstrated knowledge, skills, and abilities.
- Identifying and meeting soldiers' needs is an essential task for noncommissioned officers. We must stay in touch with the needs of today's soldiers and make every attempt to provide them with the things they need. We must also make sure we understand the fine line between wants and needs.
- Leaders have to know their soldiers well enough to foresee problems and tackle those problems before other things mask them.
- Sometimes, those whose charter is to help leaders

don't do a good job of it. Be smart and have them react to you, because you don't have time to react to them on frivolous issues and lead soldiers at the same time.

- Knowing your soldiers begins with knowing where they come from and what impact that has on their values and character.
- Sometimes, the people we lead are our army civilians. We must know and understand them and treat them with the same dignity and respect with which we treat our soldiers.

CHAPTER SEVEN
RESPECT AND REWARD THEM

Our soldiers deserve to be treated with the same dignity and respect we want for our families and ourselves. When they cover that extra mile and demonstrate exceptional commitment, they deserve to be rewarded.

It Sounded Different When My Son Said "Hooah"

He that will have his son have respect for him and his orders, must himself have a great reverence for his son. —*John Locke*

In October 1996, at Fort Jackson, South Carolina, I watched my son graduate from basic combat training. After the ceremony, I asked him how he was feeling. He responded, "Hooah, Dad." "Hooah" sounded different to me, somehow, than it did when other young men and women his age said it.

I've spent many of my years in the army training and taking care of soldiers. I guess I never really thought about the amount of trust America's mothers and fathers place in the noncommissioned officers who care for their sons and daughters. When I looked at Private Pendry and heard him say "Hooah," everything took on a different hue.

Training and caring for soldiers had always been important to me. Now it was even more so. I looked at my son's drill sergeants differently than I had before, with a father's eyes. That put a whole different perspective on everything, let me tell you.

I reflected on my days as a drill sergeant. "Hooah" wasn't a very common term among trainees in 1980. Every drill sergeant had his own favorite, I guess. "Yes, drill sergeant," and "No, drill sergeant," worked for me. When getting those responses from soldiers, I never looked at them as sons or daughters. They were raw material, and I had eight weeks to turn them into usable products for the army while weeding out the defective ones to send back home.

I wonder now: If I had looked at them more from a father's perspective, would I have worked harder to salvage those who were sent home? No one wants to see his or her children fail at anything. I guess that answers my question.

Would it have made any difference in my approach to training? Probably not, because a standard can't be compromised. But I'm sure it would have made me take a harder look at soldiers who failed certain parts of training and search for the reasons. I certainly would have looked to see if their failures were because of a failure of mine as a trainer, just as a father searches for where he may have failed his children when something goes wrong with his charges.

Looking at soldiers as sons and daughters would have made me take a closer look at everything I did. It probably also would have caused me to be a little too soft at times, just as all parents are now and again. I remember when my son was in basic training, how my wife used to worry. I would tell her that she did not have to worry about our son because army drill sergeants take better care of soldiers than most parents do. He was certainly better off there than he was in his college fraternity house.

A charter member of my positive three-meter zone used to tell his subordinate noncommissioned officers (NCOs), "When you are recommending a soldier for promotion to NCO rank, ask yourself if you would trust that person to look after your son or daughter." That certainly is the key. Our soldiers are our family; we have to treat them with the same dignity and respect with which we treat our own children. We also have to give them the same understanding and guidance. I can tell you, when your son or daughter stands in front of you wearing army green and says, "Hooah, Mom," or "Hooah, Dad," everything is going to have an added perspective.

Look at things from that perspective. Ask yourself if it's acceptable for your family to live under the same conditions as your soldiers do in garrison. Look at how they are treated and what services they get, and ask if that's good enough for your family. Ask if they are being addressed with the same dignity and respect as you would give your son or daughter.

Yep, it sure sounded different when my son said "Hooah."

Awards

Praise, recognition, a medal, a certificate, or a letter of commendation mean a great deal to a soldier.
—Field Manual 22-100, *1990*

I was in the army for ten years and was a staff sergeant before I received an award. I did have three Good Conduct Medals. I suppose you could count those. I'm not trying to gain your pity, just to illustrate a point. You would think, as many do, that a soldier with ten years of service who progressed well through the ranks probably would have accomplished something along the way that was worthy of recognition.

The job for which I received the award was different from other jobs I'd had until that point in my career. On this job, I had to learn and do many things outside my normal expertise. I also had to perform the duties of others for a long period because of personnel shortages. Later, when I read the award recommendation, it was clear that these extra things, not my routine daily duties, were the reason I received an award.

During my time in the army, the award system has gone to the extremes. It has gone from awards bloat to no awards and back again. Every time we hit an extreme, soldiers lose. We must reward soldiers when they have earned recognition. On the other hand, we have to be cautious not to make awards meaningless by passing them out too freely.

In my early days in the army, everyone had chests full of medals, mostly awards from their tours in Vietnam. And that's probably how it should have been. The problem was that too many Saigon rangers wore the same Bronze Star Medals as soldiers who left body parts in less exotic places in that country. So what's my point? It's simple: We've always had a problem with giving the right awards to the right people for the right jobs. But it's a problem NCO leadership can fix.

Sitting as the president of promotion boards and soldier recognition boards, I often ask soldiers about the awards they are wearing. More specifically, I ask them what they did to earn them. The most common response is, "I got this Army Commendation Medal for leaving . . ." The soldiers never relate getting the awards to any accomplishments other than leaving somewhere.

The reason for this is that leadership has created an expectation in soldiers that they will get awards for every tour of duty they do somewhere, regardless of whether their performance is mediocre. A leader in the army who fails to prepare a Permanent Change-of-Station (PCS) award for a soldier will probably have to answer to someone.

NCOs are frontline leaders. We have to make awards meaningful to soldiers. The only way to do that is to take away the expectation that an award is given for just doing your job. We all know of cases in which this happens. The PCS award is an example. I have known cases in which entire sections of soldiers received awards for passing recurring compliance inspections—in other words, for meeting the requirements of their jobs.

Just as importantly, though, if an NCO believes a soldier's performance merits recognition with an award, the NCO has to do justice to the recommendation and then be prepared to fight for it tooth and nail.

NCOs have to challenge the unwritten rules about awards. There are some. The PCS award is one example, but the most common is attaching rank to level of award. Soldiers must get the awards they have earned, and this must not be based on the criteria of some unwritten rules. NCOs in leadership positions must interject themselves into the award processes in their organizations. Don't fret about awards to officers, because that's not your business. Just make sure that soldier awards have NCO input on performance.

How about a war story? As one of the command sergeants major of a major command (MACOM), I sat on the awards board with the MACOM command sergeants major and others. We reviewed recommendations for awarding the Meritorious Service Medal (MSM) and higher awards. Our purpose, I guess, was to provide a sanity check and offer the commanding general recommendations.

The disparity in awards across the command was incredible. There were some special organizations in this MACOM in which a soldier could spend an entire career. One such NCO, a sergeant first class, was being recommended for a Meritorious Service Medal as a retirement award. Included in the award recommendations was a list of previous awards received. This NCO had been awarded one Army Achievement Medal (the lowest award a soldier can get in the pecking order of awards) in twenty years. One, hana, uno, eins—in twenty years.

Maybe that was all the soldier earned, but consider another case. Another NCO was leaving the command after being assigned to a prestigious unit for a little more than three years. The NCO in this case was recommended for an MSM as a PCS award. The difference was that in three years, this NCO had received seven Army Commendation Medals. That's no typo—seven medals, three years. I don't think Audie Murphy matched that rate, and he was getting shot at—a lot. End of war story.

NCOs have to put meaning into our award system. We cannot hand out medals for what amounts to coming to work on a regular basis. We have to challenge those unwritten rules and disparities in the system. Why give out MSMs for winning board competitions, then give the same medal to a master sergeant retiring with twenty-four years in the service? Go figure.

NCO leadership can make a difference when it comes to awards for enlisted soldiers. We have to start by making awards something you get for doing some work above and beyond the requirements of your job. We also have to make sure that when soldiers earn recognition, they get it. NCOs have to make sure that while soldiers in one unit receive no awards, the unit across the street isn't passing them out for making it to formation on time. One award in twenty years is probably as much of an injustice to a soldier as seven awards in three years is an injustice to the system and the army.

Promotion and Recognition Boards

Soldier recognition boards and local promotion boards are great tools for recognizing excellence and rewarding deserving soldiers. Unfortunately, across the army, these boards run the gamut from extremely challenging to mere trivial pursuit. NCOs have to make these programs effective and meaningful for soldiers; otherwise they serve no purpose. They're our programs with which to do that.

If you've been in the army for a while, I'm sure you can recount your own experiences with boards. I've had mine, and they've hit the extremes. I once reported to a promotion board (a process that was supposed to determine whether I was ready to become a noncommissioned officer) that amounted to ten minutes of trivial pursuit. The questions were a real challenge. "Who wrote 'The Star-Spangled Banner'?" "How many holes are there in a C-ration cracker?" I'm serious.

At the next board, I expected another game of trivial pursuit. Instead, I was brutalized with land-navigation problems, weapons questions, first aid, chemicals, army programs, and on and on. The command sergeant major said, "Nice try, son, but you ain't ready yet." The trivial pursuit board? I maxed that one. Two different units, two totally different approaches to the promotion board process. The shame of it is that we are doing the same things today that we did twenty-five years ago. We haven't learned our lessons.

I was a first sergeant in a battalion in which soldiers used a battalion study guide made up of lists of questions for promotion and recognition board preparation. The command sergeant major didn't allow questions to come from anywhere except the study guide. We selected soldiers to be noncommissioned officers or ordained them as our soldiers of the year because they knew the frequently inaccurate and out-of-date battalion study guide. We did not do it because they understood training, leadership, physical fitness, counseling, or anything else someone worthy of this recognition should know.

I've been on boards on which it was clear that a board member had compromised his or her integrity by providing questions to the soldiers before they came to the board. It was painfully obvious when the soldiers gave verbatim, memorized, textbook answers to those questions, but couldn't answer anything else. In the study guide battalion, this practice got so blatant that the command sergeant major would not assign areas or let board members select questions until they showed up for the board.

It's obvious that standards vary widely between units when it comes to boards. Soldiers competing for the same promotion or recognition compete under vastly different criteria.

As noncommissioned officers, we owe it to soldiers and the army to recognize and promote our best soldiers with these programs. To do that, we have to make them challenging and meaningful. The payback will be recognition and promotion of quality soldiers and NCOs who are knowledgeable and confident in their abilities.

Here are a few tips.

- Chuck trivial pursuit in the trashcan today.
- Trash any form of study guide that consists of lists of questions and answers. Forbid their use by board members. Make sure your soldiers understand that questions will not be taken from guides. (I realize that many of my peers have spent a great deal of time compiling such guides for use. Sorry, guys.)
- Develop a list of reference materials for board preparation and make sure the list and materials are provided to soldiers.
- Develop categories of questions based on how they are broken down in common skills manuals: shoot,

survive, communicate, and so forth. Then cover counseling, leadership, training, and soldier-team development.

• Move on to wear and appearance of the uniform, standards of conduct, drill and ceremonies, and customs and courtesies.

• Do away with current events questions that come from the front page of the newspaper. Just cover those things you would expect an NCO to have some knowledge about.

• Don't let board members ask questions requiring regurgitation of lists or manual and regulation numbers. Make them ask questions that cause soldiers to formulate their own answers, not to spit out memorized ones.

• Instruct board members not to ask obscure questions from notes on the table of contents page or some other such nonsense.

• Also instruct them to listen to the soldiers' answers. A soldier doesn't have to hit every pause and comma with a verbatim book answer to demonstrate knowledge of a subject.

• Have your board members submit questions for your review early enough that they can be changed if need be.

• Make board members bring their references to the board with them. If one of them brings a study guide . . .

• Make the first-line NCO supervisor accompany each soldier to the board. Hold him or her accountable when soldiers are not prepared.

NCOs own these processes. They're probably the only ones left that we totally control and influence. There are some exceptional models of how to conduct boards out there; look for them. Just figure out if you want to recognize and promote a trivial pursuit champion or a soldier or noncommissioned officer with knowledge of the things that he or she should know and understand. I know which one I would pick. I expect you will make the right choice, too.

Where's the Glory? A Rite of Passage

I stay in touch with noncommissioned officers who have shared my three-meter zone—especially the good ones. I don't put much store in their pay grades. Once they have successfully made the journey from soldiers to noncommissioned officers, their pay grades really become irrelevant. At least, in my eyes they do.

I learn as much from young NCOs as I do from old ones. I often have thought-provoking exchanges with the youngsters. They are closer in age and thinking to the soldiers I'm responsible for than I am. That makes their opinions on many issues more relevant than mine. Their opinions usually cause some critical thinking on my part. When I get their opinions on a topic, I usually try to give them a look from my perspective. What effect does that have? I'm not sure. The desired effect is that they learn to think in a broader spectrum and critically evaluate the opinions of others—the way NCOs need to think.

One of these young sergeants, of whom I think highly, asked me once, "Where's the glory in being an NCO?"

The first thoughts that came to mind were all the rhetorical answers. "We're the backbone." "We're leaders of soldiers."

Although I never verbalized those particular thoughts, knowing this sergeant as I do, I could imagine what his response would have been. "I know the creed, sergeant major; now let's get back to the question. Where is the glory in being an NCO?"

Critical thinking time again. What I did was ramble on for some time about the number of soldiers I had personally trained. I said that if they had each influenced one or two other soldiers, I had probably touched an entire division's worth by now. There was my glory, I said. He got my answer through the mail, so I never heard his response. But knowing this sergeant, I imagine it would have been something like, "I wasn't talking about your glory, sergeant major. What I mean is, how do we show a young soldier the glory in becoming a noncommissioned officer?"

I've been in places where being an NCO had different meanings. As a private in Korea, I would have given away my most valued possessions (my bell-bottomed jeans and those square-toed boots I had) just to get a look inside the NCO club. I just couldn't figure out how to get past the NCO master-at-arms who was always checking club cards.

Later on, as a staff sergeant, I had the same burning desire to visit the Top Three club. None of that was because I was particularly crazy about clubs. I just knew that if you were important enough to have your own club, you must be something special. Not knowing what was beyond the door to that club and what the Top Three did in there added a little mystique to their group. Although what was in there was unknown to outsiders, it represented a little bit of the glory associated with being a part of the group. It caused you to want to be a member.

It's not unlike being a private standing at the left end of the squad, and knowing that if you work at it, you'll someday be standing closer to the right end of that squad; maybe you'll even be the squad leader. It gives you something to look forward to: a little bit of glory.

We have to be careful about losing those distinctions that identify noncommissioned officers as a group, separate from the rest. Are we lumping enlisted personnel into a group so that there is no real distinction between sergeants and privates?

Military communities still have officers' clubs. Most, however, now have enlisted or community clubs. Typically, there is no NCO club. It's a tradition lost to the bottom line and the deglamorization of the NCO club, or any club for that matter. Before you even think it, this is not a commercial for NCO clubs. Unfortunately, some other things left along with NCO clubs, including a little bit of the glory.

The command sergeants major, for example, have stopped having NCO call at the clubs. In many places, they have stopped having it altogether. The club offered a relaxed forum to discuss soldier business and professional development, and a place to welcome new friends and bid farewell to old ones. Contrary to the beliefs of some, this was not an excuse for NCOs to get sloppy drunk once a month. Business was always conducted and concluded before any other activity started.

The most significant loss to our corps is the tradition of welcoming new noncommissioned officers into it—something else that routinely took place in the NCO clubs. We inducted them into our corps and made sure they understood how important their passage from soldier to noncommissioned officer was. They understood that they were now part of a very old fraternity—members of a time-honored corps that laid claim to being the backbone of the army.

This ensured that they understood the commitment and awesome responsibility that came with noncommissioned officers' stripes. We pounded those new stripes on and then wet them down with some of the club's beer. It wasn't a glamorous or formal ceremony, and it caused some sore shoulders and a few headaches the next day. It probably wouldn't be an acceptable practice nowadays. Pounding on and wetting down new stripes was not the real loss. The loss was a tradition that stood as a rite of passage from soldier to noncommissioned officer. Some of the glory associated with that journey is gone.

One of the charges of the noncommissioned officer is to uphold the traditions of the army. One of those traditions was the rite of passage from soldier to NCO. If there is no ceremony to induct new noncommissioned officers into the corps at your unit, then you need to ask why. A noncommissioned officer's induction ceremony is just one of those little things that tells young and old soldiers that there is some glory in becoming a noncommissioned officer. We have to protect those little things. Then young sergeants and soldiers will stop asking us, "Where's the glory?"

Where Soldiers Live

My two basic responsibilities will always be upper-most in my mind: the accomplishment of my mission and the welfare of my soldiers. —*The NCO Creed*

As we restructure our army and move toward the twenty-first century, there is much discussion about future strategy, future weapons systems, future force mix, future this, and future that. Those are great and meaningful debates for generals, senators, service secretaries, and others. For NCOs, though, the talk needs to center on the future of the ultimate weapon system. One aspect of this is how soldiers live in the garrison environment.

What about the noncareer-oriented soldiers who have replaced disgruntled conscripts as the lifeblood of our army? Career oriented or not, they are professional military people during the time that we have their services. What's in their future? Construction and renovation plans will improve the facilities in which they live during the next thirty years or so. Can we wait that long to make other needed changes?

Our thoughts on soldiers' living conditions and quality of life are slowly evolving toward parity between single and married soldiers. However, we still have a long way to go. One reason we are progressing so slowly is the way we look at the issue. Mistakenly, we make a distinction between single and married soldiers when we are trying to decide what we need in order to improve the lives of each. We have to stop categorizing our soldiers as married or single when we are trying to meet their needs. They are soldiers, and, whether married or single, share common needs.

Using a modern buzzword, we have to break a paradigm. We have to treat all soldiers the same way when it comes to where they live. Old fogies like me need to embrace some twenty-first-century notions in that regard. All soldiers have private lives that they don't care to share with others regularly when it isn't necessary. All soldiers need to identify with homes they consider theirs.

We have a lot to gain by creating this environment for our soldiers and very little, if anything, to lose. Many valuable offshoots can come from creating single-soldier communities without regard to a soldier's unit of assignment—the same way we house married soldiers. We have learned the value of having soldiers from different specialties integrated in our professional development training.

It's an enlightening experience for folks when they are finally exposed to soldiers from different backgrounds and specialties at the capstone level of the noncommissioned officer education system. It's where clerks discover that grunts can read and write. It's also where grunts find out that clerks are capable soldiers, too. We can nurture that environment by giving up on archaic ideas restricting where soldiers live because of their units of assignment.

Granted, there are instances where maintaining unit integrity is absolutely necessary to meeting mission requirements. But whatever the case, NCOs need to look hard at rules we force soldiers to abide by because of their marital status and where they live. We owe it to the soldiers to come up with the best possible living environment for them. What's best for them may not always equal what's easiest for us.

> Regardless of age or grade, soldiers should be treated as mature individuals. They are men engaged in an honorable profession and deserve to be treated as such. —*Gen. Bruce Clarke*

How soldiers live is a controversial issue in many parts of the army. Yet it shouldn't be. Regress for a minute. Think about when you were a young soldier living in the barracks. Did you like complying with specific instructions on how to conduct your life after your professional day ended? Did you really need instructions on how to line up your shoes under the bed or how to put your blankets on it? Could you have been a productive soldier without instructions on how to roll your socks and underwear, hang your clothes, and so forth?

You didn't care for that stuff. Neither did I. In fact, it was probably one of the biggest days of your military life when you moved out of that environment. It was for me. I remember thinking more than once how glad I was that I didn't live in the first sergeant's barracks anymore.

As leaders, we have to question what we accomplish with living area inspections and rules more suitable for prison inmates than professional military personnel. As the NCO leaders who enforce the rules, we have to ask: What are we teaching soldiers, and what is the point? These are the same basic questions we apply to everything that deals with soldiers.

Don't get me wrong. I was very tough on soldiers living in my barracks when I was a first sergeant. It was how my leaders treated and taught me. I thought nothing of it. It was the way we had always done it. My dad walked five miles through blizzards to school every day. Modern school buses eliminated that. Modernizing our minds a little will change how our soldiers live, too.

I have pondered some reasons offered for why we, as a group of leaders, have felt it necessary to impose restrictive standards on working adults where they live and mismanage the space meant for them to live in. Frankly, I question the validity of those reasons. Take a critical look at some that I've heard, yes, and even used myself. Ask yourself, "What's the point?" Then you decide if they make sense.

"I have to have a charge of quarters." Why? Bed checks? Clean the first sergeant's office? Hmmm?

"I need to keep all of my soldiers together in the same building. Otherwise I'll never be able to find them." Don't you keep a roster with the addresses of all your married soldiers? Are you going to demand that all your married soldiers relocate to the same neighborhood, even if there aren't enough houses for them? Does it make sense that Alpha Company has 60 soldiers living in a building designed for 200? I guess it makes as much sense as HHC housing 300 in the same-sized building.

"If I have tough standards and rules for how soldiers live in my barracks and I enforce them, I have control." Is it your barracks or their home? Do you really have control of a soldier's life at the end of the duty day? Even if you did, why would you want it? Do you want someone in control of you when you go home? Isn't it enough for you to have total control of the soldier on the job?

"I have to have strict visitation rules. How else can I control who enters the building?" What do you mean? Do you have a member of the opposite sex in your home? Did you sign her into the building? You'd better leave that door open. Also, I expect her to be out of there by 10:00 P.M. Do you really believe that every visitor you ever had in your building walked through the front door? Ha! I have visitors sign in and out of my house, too. I wouldn't want the place to turn into a brothel or a crack house.

"I can't allow soldiers to have more than a six-pack of beer in the barracks. They'll get out of control." How much does that tank cost? It has how much firepower? How about that Patriot Missile System there? By the way, whom do you trust to maintain that Apache over there?

"I have to ensure that soldiers live in a clean and healthy environment." I agree, totally. Still, does that mean you have to verify they are living in a healthy way by having daily dust-on-your-doorjamb inspections and periodic, lunatic, 3:00 A.M. health-and-welfare inspections that only net some mess hall spoons and cups?

And the champion reason: "Enforcing exact and demanding standards where soldiers live makes them pay attention to detail and causes them to perform better on their jobs." OK. Let me see if I have this straight, now. I have two options. During my personal time I may rest and recreate a little. I may sip a beer or a Pepsi and eat a little popcorn or pizza. I could also play Nintendo or watch TV. Maybe I'll just take my shoes off and rub my feet a little bit. Just like you do when you get home, Top.

Or, I can take out all of my socks and underwear and a ruler, and roll, stretch, and smooth them out until they are exactly three and six inches, respectively. Then I can place them in the prescribed place in the white towel–lined second and third drawers of my three-drawer chest. Because the top drawer already has the razor, toothbrush, shaving cream, and comb, I never use anything in it. Oh, it's also lined with a white towel.

Then I'll make a little display of my brass on a five-by-eight card. I'll perfectly align the toes of my footgear in order of boots to low quarters, military to civilian. I'll put the shower clogs on the end and make sure all are fully laced (providing they have laces) and polished. Right after that I will align all the clothes in my locker to specification. I'll measure two inches between the hangers and have all buttons facing to the left. I'll button everything as it's worn. I'll then hang them in this order: overcoat, raincoat, class-A blouse, green trousers, green shirts, long sleeves, short sleeves, battle-dress uniforms, then civilian clothes (providing there is enough room for civilian clothes).

Next, I'll tie my laundry bag to the foot of my bed. I'll use two wraps of the rope beneath an X with the right over the left and tied in a square knot on the back. Of course, no dirty laundry will be in the bag. I'll then place a clean white hand towel to the left and a clean white washcloth to the right of it. Now, once I've gotten my stylish green wool blankets hospital-corner perfect with the dust cover aligned exactly on the seventh spring, I'll sleep on the floor so I don't mess any of it up.

If I understand right, option number one will make me

a less efficient soldier. If I choose option number two, I'll be better at tank gunnery, entering a radio net, navigating point to point, writing a computer program, maintaining personnel and finance records, or whatever it is I do. It sounds perfectly logical to me. Now, as my young son might say, "Get a grip."

That's how I lived in the barracks more than twenty-five years ago. Some soldiers are living that way now (and they're not even in the confinement facility). I didn't like it worth a flip. I can't see any reason why a soldier today would like it, either.

Here's another war story. I admit it has been a slow conversion process for me. A program called Single Soldier Initiatives started when I was a first sergeant in Germany. It came across to us old soldiers as a no-inspection, no-charge-of-quarters (CQ), no-control environment. Although it was much more than that, the only thing my dinosaur associates and I heard was "no inspection, no CQ!" What in the hell can the commander in chief possibly be thinking, we wondered. On our part, it was a severe case of selective listening. We did not want to hear anything else.

It doesn't take a rocket scientist to figure out that the average military professional is a little bit of a control freak. That isn't always bad, of course. Many military situations require tight control. Is it necessary, though, to carry that control over to a soldier's home? A home is personal. Who am I to make a soldier's home reflect my personality?

At the outset of these initiatives, senior NCOs expressed common thoughts. "We will lose control of our soldiers.

Our barracks will become brothels and drug dens. They will get filthy and stay filthy. Our soldiers will become undisciplined and out of control."

I was glad to be leaving Europe and turning over the startup of that plan to someone else. Not having control of my soldiers and my barracks was something this first sergeant was certain would fail.

During the two years I was away from Europe, I kept hearing the nightmare being played out by my friends still assigned to Germany. "The buildings are absolutely filthy," I would hear. "If you inspect the barracks now, boy, you're going to have to answer to the chain of command." Everything was just as I had feared it would be. We had lost control.

Imagine my reluctance when I was asked if I wanted my first command sergeant major assignment to be right back in the battalion I had just left. It was the same battalion from which I was getting my information about the lack of control of soldiers.

When I arrived in the battalion, one of my first actions was to walk around to see just how bad off we were. I saw what they had told me I would see. Suddenly, first sergeants were happy to take me around and show me dirty—and dirty is a mild word—rundown barracks. They were pleased to say, "See, SGM, we tried to tell them this would happen. They wouldn't listen to us." It was distressing. These same first sergeants would go to great lengths to have a clean, healthy environment for their soldiers to live in. They would even border on some illegality to improve a day room or come up with something good for the soldiers.

I spent much time trying to figure out why things were in such a state and how they got there. I wondered why buildings that we had renovated five years earlier looked like they were going on twenty. That is when I really began to educate myself on the Single Soldier Initiatives program. I read what they had written over the commander in chief's signature and watched his video. I pondered it all.

Then one day, it was like someone had hit me between the eyes with a two-by-four. The reason this program wasn't working was because NCOs did not want it to work. They had taken a hands-off, negative approach that ensured the failure of the program. They were pleased to say, "I told you so." By sitting on our hands and doing nothing, we were ensuring the program's failure. We knew that. What we needed to do was adopt a positive attitude and a positive approach to making the program work.

Using my persuasive personality, I convinced the first sergeants that we needed to take a positive approach and support this program. We did. We ended with a showcase for managing soldiers' quarters. When the battalion deactivated, we turned the management over to the housing office, and the residents never knew the difference.

Positive involvement by NCOs was the only reason we were successful. We made sure everyone had a clear picture of the commander's intent, which was basic. We were to bring single soldiers' quality of life on par with that of married soldiers to the greatest extent possible.

The most significant change we could make was in how we managed their housing. We knew what the soldiers wanted. They wanted elimination of rules that applied to them just because they were single and living in the barracks. They wanted what we want: privacy, no unnecessary inspections, and freedom to decorate their homes as they saw fit. We knew why the program had failed in the past. We did not plan for it to work. A lack of involvement by NCOs and other leadership demonstrated that. End of war story.

There are a few lessons here for NCO leaders. NCOs can cause almost any plan or idea to work or fail. Remember attitudes? NCOs owe it to soldiers to give them a living environment that's best for them, as opposed to being easiest for NCOs to manage. Remember our creed, "My two basic responsibilities . . . the accomplishment of my mission and the welfare of my soldiers"?

Finally, rigid and restrictive standards where soldiers live do have their place. The place is where soldiers learn the value of following rules, living up to prescribed, exacting standards, and paying attention to the littlest details. It's where soldiers learn the army ethic, conformity, teamwork, and all the skills important to being a soldier. That place is basic combat training. Not where professional working adults—soldiers—live.

Summary

- Our soldiers are sons and daughters of America. Their care is entrusted to the army's noncommissioned officer corps. They deserve to be taught, treated, and led with the same respect and dignity we would show our own children.
- Awards are important to soldiers. It's just as im-

portant that noncommissioned officers ensure awards are not made meaningless by lessening the criteria for which they are given. We owe it to deserving soldiers to make sure they get awards, and we have to be prepared to fight like hell to get them.

- Promotion and soldier recognition boards are very important. Ensure that they are thorough, challenging, and meaningful.

- Becoming a noncommissioned officer is special. We must make a special effort to distinguish between soldiers and noncommissioned officers and must make an event of welcoming new NCOs into the corps.

- We have to make an effort to provide our soldiers with the best possible living conditions to make up for those times when we can't. Then we have to go to great lengths to ensure that they are treated as mature adults where they live.

CHAPTER EIGHT
MOTIVATE THEM

Motivation is the cause of action. It gives soldiers the will to do what you know must be done to accomplish the mission. —Field Manual 22-100, *1990*

What Really Motivates Soldiers?

What motivates soldiers? I've sure had a lot of theories flung at me trying to answer that question—self-esteem theories, needs theories, rewards theories, and probably eight or ten more that I either can't or don't care to remember. The answer could be any or a combination of all of these. I expect the answer lies with leaders—positive, caring leaders who show soldiers genuine concern for their problems, needs, and families. A leader who motivates, willingly shares difficult times with soldiers, passes credit to them when they succeed, and takes responsibility when they fail.

Another war story. When I became a first sergeant, I found what I viewed as a problem with how the unit managed the weight control and special fitness training programs. The programs were being managed in accordance with the applicable regulations (that's bureaucrat for "by the book"). They were excellent programs in that regard. A lot of soldiers had been on the programs for a long time. Most should have, by all rights, been discharged from the army for not meeting the standard.

After I examined the program, it was difficult for me to recommend to the commander that the soldiers be discharged. The truth is, I felt downright uncomfortable making that recommendation. A lot had been done to these soldiers, but from my perspective, not very much had been done for them. The program consisted of telling them their weight and body fat percentage, how much to lose, and by what date to lose it. If these soldiers had had the proper habits and knowledge about nutrition, the right kind of physical training habits, and the self-motivation to follow through, they wouldn't have been in the predicament they were in.

We started them off with proper counseling on nutrition and fitness. Then we began a well-designed physical training program. My personally leading the program every evening had a positive effect on the soldiers and on me. I did every exercise with them and ran every run they did. Every soldier in the program was ultimately successful in meeting the army standard and staying in the army. That convinced me that personal interest and involvement motivate soldiers to want to succeed.

One by one, as they met the standard, these soldiers continued with the evening program. The soldiers named their program Challenge Physical Training. They challenged others to participate with them. It was a case of perpetual motivation. These soldiers were proud of their accomplishments, and they became the best motivators for others trying to meet the standard. At times as many as fifty soldiers, including other leaders, participated in this program, of whom only about ten were required to do so. Ultimately, all the original soldiers enrolled in the Challenge Physical Training program were successful and damn proud of themselves. Some had been on the weight control program for more than a year. End of war story.

So, what motivates soldiers? It is leaders who take a personal interest in their situation and their needs and are willing to sacrifice a little to help them out. That one achievement affected everything these soldiers did: how they performed in other aspects of their jobs, how others viewed them, and how they viewed themselves. A few leaders who cared motivated these soldiers. There is your answer. Positive, caring leaders willing to share the hard times motivate soldiers.

> From most of us you can expect . . . courage to match your courage, guts to match your guts, endurance to match your endurance, motivation to match your motivation, esprit to match your esprit, a desire for achievement to match your desire for achievement. You can expect a love of God, a love of country and a love of duty to match your love of God, your love of country and your love of duty. We won't mind the heat if you sweat with us, and we won't mind the cold if you shiver with us. —*Sgt. Maj. John G. Stepanek*

Not too long ago, I went on a staff ride to the Gettysburg battlefield. That alone can be an intense, sobering experience. I listened intently as our professional historian described the repeated attacks by the Confederates on the position of the Federals' 20th Maine on Little Round Top. There were five attacks directly up a rocky hill against an enemy in the defense. The attacks came close, but never succeeded in capturing the top of the hill.

I wondered what motivated those Confederate soldiers to continue to press attack after unsuccessful attack—what motivated soldiers who had just force-marched twenty-five miles, many with no shoes. That was twenty-five miles in July heat, and they didn't even get water before they were put into the battle.

On the other side, what motivated the valiant stand of the soldiers of the 20th Maine? What motivated them to stand and fight when they could have easily turned tail and run to safety? When they were dangerously low on ammunition, what motivated them to fix their bayonets, leave the relative security of their defensive positions, and sweep down Little Round Top's rocky slope to break the back of the Confederate attack? Self-esteem, fear, needs, rewards?

I heard a similar account when the action on Cemetery Hill was described. While standing on the Federal positions on Cemetary Ridge and looking out at more than a mile of open space crossed by Confederate soldiers during Pickett's Charge, I asked myself the same question. What could possibly motivate soldiers to press an attack into the face of an artillery firing canister by an enemy in strong defensive positions? What type of leader did it take to motivate soldiers to press on through the heat of the day, confusion, smoke, and deafening noise? I couldn't imagine what words a leader could speak that would motivate soldiers to march shoulder to shoulder, unwavering, into such an attack.

Then, as the historian described to us where and how Confederate General Armistead had been fatally wounded, the answer became clear. While leading his element in the charge, he had advanced beyond the first line of Federal artillery to within meters of the main Union force when he was killed. He had affixed his distinctive black felt hat to the tip of his sword as a signal to his soldiers while challenging them to follow him. He led his soldiers knowing that if he was successful, he might be responsible for the death of his dearest friend, General Hancock, leading the soldiers on the other side.

It wasn't words that motivated the soldiers on either side of this epic and historic battle. It wasn't anything leaders said. It was what leaders did. They motivated their men by getting out in front and leading them into the face of danger. Leaders that are motivated and willing to face danger with their soldiers motivate the soldiers. It causes me to wonder about some of the accounts I've read of commanders in Vietnam, leading from a couple of miles above the fight—from their helicopters—and getting medals for it, too.

What Doesn't Motivate Soldiers?

The short answer to that question is anything other than positive, caring leaders. "Y'all better get motivated or there is going to be hell to pay!" How often have you heard that one? Probably a lot more often than you can remember.

I would rather try to persuade a man to go along, because once I have persuaded him he will stick. If I scare him, he will stay as long as he is scared, and then he is gone. —*Gen. Dwight Eisenhower*

Fear is not a motivator. Threat of punishment is not a motivator. Motivated soldiers work to do the best job they can because they know that their leaders will take care of them and that good, positive things always come from doing their best. Motivated soldiers are a product of that type of positive environment.

Soldiers working in a fear environment will do only what is necessary to make sure the threat is not carried out. They will have no desire to do more than that, because for their efforts they are offered threats. If they are constantly threatened, they will never give their leaders more than mediocre performances. Why should they? A negative, fear-backed environment does not motivate soldiers.

How Do You Measure Motivation?

"Hear how good they sound? That's a motivated bunch there, boy." What exactly does motivation sound like, anyway? "It's loud and fired up." How did you get them so motivated? "We did push-ups until they couldn't do any more; now they're motivated." Is this motivation or fear of doing push-ups until they drop? My bet is on the latter. The decibel level of a formation of soldiers can be an indicator of their motivation, but only to the extent that it's backed up by performance.

How do you measure motivation? Look at individual soldiers. Do they display a lot of pride in their appearance? Are they proud to be in the unit to which they are assigned? Take a look at the unit. Are all the soldiers proud of the unit? Does the appearance of the unit area support that? Look at measurable standards. Is the unit above average? Are unit retention objectives met? That's how you measure motivation.

Maybe I Ain't Gonna Do It Anymore

By leaders sharing in the unit's day-to-day experiences, always available to their soldiers, they communicate their example as quality leaders and soldiers to all unit members.
—Field Manual 22-102, *1987*

I didn't run the Army Ten-Miler the last time it came up. Oh, I was ready, registered, and trained. Running ten miles is not a big deal to me. This time, however, I couldn't decide for whom I was running, what had motivated me to do it before, or why I was running now. And it's not just running; it's everything.

I've participated in a lot of these events over the years, and I have the knees, hips, and other failing body parts as proof. The question I had a devil of a time resolving this time was why. Why was I out there running? I had no great love of running, so why?

I pondered the question for a while and didn't like the answers I kept coming up with. I concluded that maybe I had been running in these high-visibility events and participating in others for the wrong reasons. It's tough to admit, but my focus was more on which high rollers might notice me than on sharing time with soldiers. Sharing the time and experience with them is important to being accepted by them as a leader.

You see, you don't accept the troops; they were here first. They accept you, and when they do, you'll know. They won't beat drums, wave flags, or carry you off the drill field on their shoulders, but you'll know. —*Sgt. Maj. John G. Stepanek*

The last time I ran the ten-miler, I saw the sergeant major of the army, the chief of staff of the army, a lot of other high rollers, and many of my peers. The really sad part is that I can't recall which of my soldiers I saw. After my soul searching was over, I decided that if I wasn't doing it with and for soldiers, I was motivated by the wrong purpose.

Just as leader actions motivate soldiers, leaders must make soldiers their motivators. Soldiers have to be our focus and our reason for participating in such events—not a bunch of old sergeants major trying to impress one another. We need to give our time to soldiers and try to inspire them.

As soldiers share common goals, interests, and experiences, they feel pride in shared experiences and begin to develop a sense of comradeship.
—Field Manual 22-102, *1987*

We shouldn't wait for major staged, high-visibility events to do that, because if we do, we're likely to miss out on other important times. And you know what? Maybe I ain't gonna do that anymore.

Summary

- Soldiers are motivated by the actions of leaders, not by the words of leaders. They are motivated by positive, caring leaders who are out in front sharing the hard and dangerous times with them.
- Soldiers are not motivated by fear. Soldiers driven by fear will perform until the fear is removed—and then it will only be a minimum performance.
- We also motivate soldiers, and them us, by participating in events together. We should never wait for high-visibility events to share our time with soldiers.

  A morning run with a company of soldiers is much more rewarding for you and motivating for them than participation in all the high-visibility events there are.

CHAPTER NINE
TRAIN THEM

To lead an untrained people to war is to throw them
away. —*Confucius*

A Matter of Survival

Training is not free. It always costs something—money,
time, or people. It can be cheap in terms of resources, or
it can cost a lot. Whatever the cost, it will never equal the
potential cost of not training.

Noncommissioned officers (NCOs) are the army's principal trainers, charged with its most important aspect—
individual training. Individual training is the foundation
for everything in the army. No commander can complete
a mission, training or real, without soldiers well trained
in individual skills.

There are many approaches to teaching individual soldier skills. Some hit the mark and some don't. Whenever
individual training programs fail to get the job done, it's
usually for the same reasons. They lack variety; do not
challenge soldiers physically or mentally; are poorly
planned, prepared, and presented; or do not put soldiers
in a scenario that reinforces the skill. Soldiers need to understand and experience the purpose for their training.

In commands or organizations where it's possible, Sergeant's Time Training has been a popular approach. The program gives squad-level noncommissioned officers several hours per week to train team and individual tasks. When used properly, it's very effective, but it has to be tied to a purpose. The purpose comes from the mission, using the collective-task-to-individual-task process. The process and purpose of the training is framed in a context that soldiers can relate to and understand. They see where their task fits into the bigger picture. Soldiers have to know that their ability is the foundation for every other action in the unit, and that their inability to perform critical individual tasks leads to unit-mission failure.

Too often, in combat service support, headquarters, staff agencies, or garrison-type units, these programs fail because they get stuck in the common task test rut. They become repetitive, boring, common skills training that may be worse than no training at all, or maybe forgotten altogether. Noncommissioned officers in these organizations have to know how to use the template provided in *Field Manual 25-101, Battle Focused Training*, to determine which individual skills to teach.

You must plan training so that your soldiers are challenged and learn. Some leaders find conducting training is threatening and embarrassing. When they present boring instruction, their soldiers balk at repetitive training on skills they have already mastered. When the leader discovers he has nothing else to teach he reverts back to using his position power. He accuses good soldiers of having poor attitudes and tries to order soldiers to act interested in monotonous training. The result of this scenario is strong unity among soldiers but disrespect for the leader. —Field Manual 22-100, *1990*

I don't know any leader who would assume that a combat-arms soldier knows everything about a complex weapon system. However, we readily assume that because a soldier has a computer on his or her desk, he or she knows how to use it properly. It's a foolish assumption made every day, which would never be made in an environment where lives could be at stake. I've seen much expensive equipment performing like overpriced typewriters because soldiers lacked the skills to use it any other way—skills that a training plan can provide. That same mentality transfers to other training, and we assume that soldiers know their survival skills when they don't.

Our Battle Focused Training doctrine is a superior training system. Noncommissioned officers have to know it, not because it tells us how to teach, but because it tells us how to determine what to teach. We have to clearly understand our role in the training system used by our army.

NCOs have to use initiative and imagination in situations in which the field manual and master training plan don't answer all the questions. As an NCO, you will eventually be in an environment in which you would get as much response speaking in a lost language as you get to the questions, "What's our mission-essential task list? When's our quarterly training briefing? Can I see the long-range training calendar?" You may also find yourself in a place where you have no organic equipment, no unit weapons, soldiers with no individual equipment, and no training facilities. What do you do then? Do you just forget about individual skills?

Many do, unfortunately, and you could also—if you were 100 percent certain that another one of those Grenada, Panama, Desert Storm, Somalia, Haiti, or Bosnia things wasn't going to come along. You would also have to be certain that the soldiers for whom you were responsible were never going to leave the safe, secure place where they were. With those guarantees, you could safely forget it. Otherwise, you need to do some stuff that normally isn't very popular in such an environment.

A deployable organization with a war mission is the ideal place to apply the framework of Battle Focused Training. You have a mission statement developed to support the next-higher-level unit mission. Developed to support the mission is a mission-essential task list. Your next level of command has identified for you, from your mission-essential tasks, battle tasks that are critical to mission accomplishment at their level.

Supporting the mission-essential tasks, unit-collective tasks are identified all the way down to the squad. Supporting the squad-collective tasks are crew and team tasks and drills. The individual soldier, well trained in his or her individual and job skills, provides the foundation for that pyramid. Without this, the simplest team task cannot be performed.

In organizations in which you perform your mission daily, soldier training sometimes suffers. It suffers because these organizations do not have training or training management as a part of their focus. Usually, in organizations like these, no one has taken the time to put the mission into words. Without that base statement, the organizations are unable to identify what tasks they must be able to do to accomplish their missions. They are on a trip that has neither a roadmap nor a destination.

Battle Focused Training is designed with war fighting in mind, because that is what an army does. However, the framework for the training it lays out can be easily applied to all organizations. In fact, it makes an excellent management tool for cutting out unnecessary, redundant tasks and identifying skills in which individuals need training to support the mission. Noncommissioned officers in support and administrative organizations have to adopt this framework and tailor it to suit their needs.

As an installation command sergeant major, I spent time with the staff and tenants of the installation developing our installation management action plan (training plan). We spent a week rewriting our mission to support the major command's mission, writing our vision (training goal), and identifying our key business drivers (mission-essential tasks) that supported the mission. We paid good money to a civilian contractor to be our conductor during this process, when we could have just followed the framework of Battle Focused Training for free. In fact, that's exactly what our civilian contractor, a retired army colonel, did. He just civilianized some terms to make the process more palatable to our predominantly civilian staff.

Developing a training plan for an organization is not hard. Even without the support of the key players in an organization, a noncommissioned officer can develop and carry out such a plan for a section's enlisted soldiers, no matter what the size of the organization, just by following the framework of Battle Focused Training. Just as quickly as we find ways to give soldiers time off when they need it, we can develop training plans for them. View your daily mission as the battle, and it's easy from there. The improved efficiency of the organization will cause important folks to ask, "How did you do that?"

What your plan may be lacking in such an environment is the opportunity to reinforce individual combat and survival skills. In deployable organizations that use battle-focused training management, individual combat and survival skills are reinforced as part of the training routine. If your soldiers are sitting inside the catacombs of the Pentagon, after three years their survival skills are about equal to those of initial-entry trainees just off the street. Noncommissioned officers have to prevent this from happening. How, you ask? It's not easy, I assure you.

The first step for NCOs is to commit to spending some time looking after soldiers and their training. No one else is going to, and soldiers don't know how. The officers in these organizations focus on other things, as they have to. Frankly, they will never worry about soldier training again, unless they are fortunate enough to become commanders. It's just a fact of life.

NCOs, though, have an obligation to soldiers. It's in our creed, and we have to be willing to dedicate the time and effort to meet it. The obligation is encompassed by our two basic responsibilities—accomplishment of the mission and welfare of the soldiers.

The starting point for a survival skills training plan is the *Soldiers' Manual for Common Tasks,* skill levels one through four. You do not have to take soldiers away from their colonels for more than an hour or so per week to keep them current on soldier skills.

There is no officer I can think of who would deny a soldier the opportunity to train in those skills, especially if you have already established that you can improve the efficiency of an organization just by developing a mission-supporting training plan for the soldiers. Granted, some will whine about it, but they will eventually go along if you continue to insist—and you must insist. The few who will resist such training have long forgotten what their profession entails, anyway. Many would go along for training themselves if they weren't afraid of taking heat from their own bosses or ribbing from their peers.

Every soldier in the army has a first sergeant. The first sergeant is the place to start in developing a survival skills training program for soldiers. The first sergeant will let you know about training aids, facilities, and maybe even some instructors. If you don't get the support you think you should from the first sergeant, every soldier also has a command sergeant major. The help you need to regreen your soldiers is there. It's not going to come looking for you, though.

Convincing folks of the importance of helping soldiers in a relaxed environment to maintain combat and survival skills is not an easy task. It's not easy because sitting in a nice climate-controlled office it's hard to picture the need for such training, especially if it might take some time away from the routine.

Noncommissioned officers have to insist that this time be given to soldiers. Continue to remind the leadership that although they may never find themselves in a survival situation again, that guarantee cannot be given to junior enlisted people. One or two hours per week of a soldier's time is not going to cripple any organization. You would be hard-pressed to find a soldier or leader who doesn't waste that much time in a week. Use your imagination with soldier training. It can be accomplished in many ways, and you don't always have to get up and leave your place of duty to do it.

Your other challenge is convincing soldiers in this environment that such training is necessary. When soldiers show a lack of interest or start coming up with reasons why they can't participate, then maybe they're candidates for reassignment to line units. Tell it to them just like that. Make them understand that there are many soldiers in those units who would relish the opportunity to do a tour where they are, and who would never question the necessity of survival skills training.

Training Officers

Let's get something straight right up front in this discussion. Noncommissioned officers don't teach officers how to be officers. Other officers do that. If I were an officer, I would be just as offended by an NCO trying to teach me how to be an officer as I am now when an officer tries to teach me how to be an NCO. "I don't know a damn thing about flying airplanes, but come on over here and let me teach you how to fly one." Get my point?

I've heard senior officers go on and on about how particular NCOs made them successful officers. Those NCOs probably did make contributions. They probably taught the officers a lot about soldiers, adding all the little details to fill in the blanks left by their officer training. But officers in Reserve Officer Training Corps (ROTC) units, West Point, or Officer's Candidate School taught them how to be officers, and that training continued with their commanders and other officers. If all of those folks did their jobs right then, the officers were taught that they had a lot to learn about soldiers and taking care of them, and they learned that from NCOs.

Young lieutenants, like young privates, are very impressionable. The major difference between the two is their pay grade. One usually comes with a college education, too—although nowadays, that's not always a difference.

I came up in an army in which a lot of officers had lost their trust in the NCO corps, mainly because the corps had been decimated by Vietnam. What was left for these officers was a corps of young NCOs with less experience than they had, or old ones who had lost faith in them and the army and had given up.

This was a first and lasting impression of the NCO corps for many of these officers. Many of them progressed through the army without ever fully regaining their trust in NCOs. I knew some of them as commanders, and even generals. Their feelings about NCOs were apparent in their actions. Maybe because of that lack of trust, they never learned the most important lesson officers must learn from NCOs.

Officers don't know about enlisted soldiers, because most have never been enlisted soldiers. Some may have had time as enlisted soldiers, but none of them have the enlisted experience you do if you are a platoon sergeant. In jobs in which NCOs and officers work together directly—as platoon sergeant and platoon leader, first sergeant and commander, or command sergeant major and commander—the experience level in years is usually not equal until sometime around the brigade level. The NCO almost always has more years. In all cases, the NCO has more years with soldiers. Unlike the officer, the NCO has been an enlisted soldier for a lifetime.

So what's the lesson? The most critical lesson NCOs have to teach officers is to never decide an enlisted issue without consulting a trusted NCO. Without an NCO's perspective, it's not likely an officer will make the best decision. Officers should never decide enlisted issues without the benefit of input from the people who have daily contact with soldiers. NCOs have to teach them that.

Sometimes NCOs hold positions of trust in which they have to make hard decisions—decisions that might impact an individual's career, and that have much larger ramifications across a unit or even the army. When an NCO has to make such tough decisions—for example, to relieve a substandard NCO from his or her duties—it's not easy. If an officer takes action to overturn one of those decisions without consulting a trusted enlisted advisor or discussing it with the NCO who had to make the decision, he or she never learned that critical lesson. This has happened; otherwise it wouldn't warrant discussion.

Any officer, regardless of rank, who believes that an

NCO takes lightly the action to relieve another NCO and would do it improperly and without justification is terribly mistaken. If the officer then overturns that action without even discussing it with the NCO who had to make the tough call, the officer has compounded that mistake and risks losing the confidence of the NCOs and soldiers who made the officer successful in the first place.

I know I'm being repetitive, but sometimes you need to be. NCOs have only one lesson to teach officers. Before officers make decisions about soldiers or make decisions that impact the enlisted force, they must seek the opinions of senior enlisted soldiers. That's the only training officers need from NCOs. And they aren't always getting it. That's an NCO failure.

I ran across an example of this one day. Maybe it was just an honest mistake or omission, or maybe it wasn't. When I went to the command sergeants major course, I received an article written by Cmd. Sgt. Maj. John W. Gillis, "Tips for the New Battalion Commander on the Utilization of His Battalion Command Sergeant Major." In the article, Command Sergeant Major Gillis gives a lot of sound advice to new commanders and provides them with a list of dos and don'ts for dealing with their command sergeants major. The first thing on Command Sergeant Major Gillis's list of things to do for new commanders is

DO advise your command sergeant major, in private, that there is no one between you in the chain of command. This is a basic point but must be stated early to provide a clear understanding for both of you. Advise your staff officers, also privately, that the command sergeant major's position is that of a special enlisted advisor to you with direct access and accountability to you.

I thought that was sound advice for commanders, and it still is. It's a point I've made sure to clarify with every commander with whom I've served as a first sergeant or command sergeant major. As of this writing, that's eight commanders.

One of my commanders, on returning from the pre-command course, gave me a copy of the course's version of Command Sergeant Major Gillis's article. The first thing I noticed was that nowhere in the article did it credit Command Sergeant Major Gillis with writing it in the first place. That struck me as odd. Out of curiosity, I pulled out the copy of Command Sergeant Major Gillis's article I had received at the Sergeants Major Academy and compared it with the one my commander had received at the officers' course.

In addition to not giving Command Sergeant Major Gillis credit for his writing, there was another glaring omission in my commander's copy. It was the first thing on Command Sergeant Major Gillis's "do" list, quoted previously. This may have been just an honest omission, or maybe even an unchecked clerical error; or maybe it was intentionally left out.

Again, officers need to learn one important lesson from NCOs. It now appears that they must also be periodically reminded of it. If they learn that lesson early and remember it, then discussions like this one will not be necessary.

Officers must learn that in most jobs they will ever have in the army, especially troop-leading jobs, there will always be a need to take into confidence NCOs they trust, whose advice they must seek before making decisions that have to do with soldiers. To do otherwise is a clear example of an officer who never truly learned the art of leading soldiers. That officer never learned the most basic lesson that he or she needed to learn. And that lesson has to be taught to officers by NCOs.

If you have an officer teammate who does not seek your advice before making decisions that impact enlisted soldiers, you are obligated to tell that officer about it. If you tell the officer and he or she still refuses to seek your advice in the future, then the officer either doesn't trust you personally or has never learned this lesson. Either way, I suggest you find a new officer for whom to work. Because if the first is true, you will fail; if the second is true, the officer will fail, and you won't be able to help.

The Investigation Box

I decided to put this section here because it's a good follow up to the preceding one. It adds some emphasis to the importance of establishing communication with your officer teammate so that the officer does seek your advice.

Some leaders paint their units into a dangerous box: the investigation box. Three-meter soldiers thrive in units trapped in the investigation box. These soldiers know that when a unit is stuck in the investigation box, the right type of complaint will cause leaders to be dragged through the mud. In the investigation box, this happens, while the complainers are not held accountable for anything they have said. It's a humiliating experience for leaders. It causes them to wonder why they should bother with jobs or issues that put them into such predicaments. That's a dangerous box for a unit to be in.

When leaders tire of being investigated, the result can be bad for the unit. Leaders fearing the trauma of investigations if they enforce army standards or regulations may choose not to do that anymore. Where does that leave the army?

In the investigation box, you hear, "Let's investigate it so we can say we thoroughly looked into it if we need to." That's a Charlie Yankee Alpha approach to leading. Leaders taking that approach are making a serious mistake, because it adversely impacts subordinate leaders—mostly the NCO leaders found in the three-meter zone. When something adversely affects them, it adversely affects the entire unit.

Leaders need not have everything investigated. They must take time themselves to examine the substance of complaints and make their own decisions about what should or should not be investigated. They can never rubber-stamp the recommendations of lawyers and others. A leader who does that is not leading. The lawyer, who has never led anything, is.

When a leader delegates leadership responsibility like that, the leader creates an unhealthy leadership environment and risks some losses. First, the demonstrated lack of trust in subordinate leaders will gain only a reciprocal lack of trust. Subordinate leaders will copy the leader's actions as they paint their pieces of the army into the investigation box. Most serious, though, is that the subordinate leaders may avoid making decisions and enforcing standards if they expect to be investigated for doing so.

During the 1970s, our NCO corps gave up on standards and discipline. One of the reasons those NCOs gave up was that whenever they busted a barracks full of dope smokers, the dopers ended up getting off while the NCOs were called "old lifers" and vilified for violating the rights of the dopers.

NCOs didn't need classes on search and seizure and probable cause; they needed support to help them cauterize a festering sore. They knew what was wrong in their three-meter zones, and they tried to fix it. Dope was wrong, and they didn't need a urinalysis or a bogus health-and-welfare inspection to figure out who was using it. When they went after dopers the way they knew how, the system and their own leaders shot them in the face with chicken-shit investigations. And the dopers walked away.

NCOs can counteract this pressure. It's simple; first, do things right, aboveboard, and by the book. If you do that, then investigations be damned.

Second, if you're a decent NCO, you know your soldiers. You certainly know them better than any leader in a position to initiate an investigation. That's in your creed. Before a leader makes a decision to investigate, make sure he or she has your opinion right alongside the lawyer's. (If you have convinced the officer that the most basic lesson in the soldier business is seeking enlisted advice, then the officer will listen.)

In your opinion, explain what the rules are and what others may not know. Tell the officer all about the complainer and all about the person the complaint is made against. Say whether you think an investigation should go forward. Remind the officer of the ramifications of an investigation. If you are a solid NCO, the officer you are advising trusts you. Don't try to make the decision for the officer. Just pass on everything you know about the people and the problem in the most unbiased, nonsugar-coated way you can. Then tell the officer that he or she does have the option to say no.

If the leader listens to everything you have to say before making a decision, then you are obligated to support his or her decision. If the officer makes the decision without seeking your advice, you are obligated to tell the officer where he or she failed. Do that, and then find a new officer to work for. In that case, get out of that officer's investigation box.

Summary

- Noncommissioned officers are the army's principal trainers. We shoulder the responsibility for the most important piece of training: the individual soldier. If we fail, the army fails. NCOs must understand army training doctrine and be prepared to meet soldier training needs in all types of environments.
- We don't have much to do with the training of officers in how to be officers. Other officers do that. We do owe it to them to teach them about soldiers. The most important lesson we have to teach officers is that they must involve noncommissioned of-

ficers in decisions involving enlisted issues. If they forget that, we are obligated to keep reminding them of it.

- Investigations are a serious and potentially dangerous business. Make sure one is warranted before starting it. Leaders who grow tired of investigations will also grow tired of leading.

CHAPTER TEN
PHYSICALLY TRAIN THEM

The costly lessons learned by Task Force Smith in Korea are as important today as ever. If we fail to prepare our soldiers for their physically demanding wartime tasks, we are guilty of paying lip service to the principle of "train as you fight." Our physical training programs must do more for our soldiers than get them ready for the semiannual Army Physical Fitness Test (APFT). —Field Manual 21-20, *1992*

Throughout my time in the army, I have been a strong advocate of physical fitness; sometimes, I've even been considered a mite radical. Before you read the rest of the book, however, it's important to me that you as a leader or potential leader understand a couple of things.

- First, as leaders, we are obligated to enthusiastically support and enforce the rules, regulations, and standards that we are given. That's our charge. If we don't do that, then we have violated the most basic rule of leading. If you come away after reading these chapters believing that I want you to disregard a regulation or not enforce a current standard, you're mistaken and you've missed the point.

- We have another obligation as important as following the rules that I also feel strongly about. That obligation is to ensure that fitness and weight control programs, or any other soldier programs for that matter, focus on the soldiers and not the unit PT test averages or the correctness of the weight control program paperwork. If we fail that obligation, we have violated the second most basic rule of leading: taking care of people.
- There is one final obligation I want you to consider as you read the rest of the book. A leader must be creative and imaginative in developing fitness and weight control programs. You must also be candid enough to share your opinions on these and other soldier programs. That's what causes us to think, and that's how we get better.

Can't Get Enough of That PT

Talk about an evolution. (That sounds like a Beatles song, doesn't it?) In 1971, when I got my first dose of army physical fitness training (PT), it was a lot different from what you see units doing today. We had economical physical fitness uniforms, too. We grounded our headgear, unbloused our trousers, and pulled our shirttails out.

We had cotton fatigue uniforms then. We didn't have big, baggy battle-dress uniform shirts to camouflage our bellies. The quartermaster laundry would put so much starch in those uniforms, we had to break the trouser legs and shirtsleeves apart just to get them on. I guess that's where the phrase "breaking starch" came from. They looked like hell after you'd been wearing them for a few minutes, especially if you were running around in the Fort Ord fog like I was.

But, back to PT. We had three conditioning drills in those days, with twelve exercises in each drill. We kept them right up through the early 1980s, too. Then some smart guys somewhere figured out that all that twisting, squatting, bending, jerking, and contorting we called exercise was doing as much harm to our bodies as it was doing them good. The same guys also said we couldn't or shouldn't run in combat boots anymore, either. Of course, they made those changes after I had finished eight weeks of all three conditioning drills and daily five-milers in drill sergeant school.

It's odd, but I don't recall ever seeing a tennis shoe profile before we started actually running in tennis shoes. I do recall low quarters profiles. Funniest thing you've ever seen. If the uniform of the day was fatigues, that was what you wore, even if you had to wear your low quarters.

I can only recall doing four exercises in basic training, unless you call running up and down the stairs for midnight fire drills exercise. They were the push-up, the squat thrust, the body twist, and a work of art called the eight-count push-up. This was a squat thrust with a four-count push-up in the middle.

Just in case you are too young to know what a squat thrust is, I'll explain. The squat thrust starts at the position of attention. On the first count, you squat and place your hands on the ground in about the same position you would if you were preparing to do a push-up. On the second count, you thrust your legs back and assume the front-leaning rest position. Just picture yourself getting into and out of the front-leaning rest position as a moderate four-count exercise. Funny how the drill sergeants never seemed to tire—of watching us do those exercises.

I'm not sure that the point of physical fitness in those days was to make you physically fit—at least not the way we were doing it. When I was lying there in that Fort Ord sand, unable to raise my legs again on the short count of "Ooooooone . . . twoo . . . threeeeee . . . four . . ." of the body twist, I didn't see the physical training benefit of being called bubble-butt and having my ancestry questioned by the drill sergeants.

Basic training was my last exposure to organized physical training for a long, long time. In advanced individual training (AIT), we had a first sergeant who looked like he might tip the scales at about 400 pounds. He would wheeze walking up the steps into the mess hall, puffing on his cigar, and cussing out privates. (We had mess halls before we had dining facilities, too.) We had a platoon sergeant, I think, but he never led any PT.

We did have to take a PT test to get out of AIT. We had a five-event test then: the horizontal ladder (monkey bars), one minute of bent-leg sit-ups, the inverted crawl (obviously thought up by the genius who came up with the high-jumper), and the run-dodge-and-jump (which was exactly what you did—you ran, dodged barricades, jumped a ditch, turned around, and did it again). That was one event I could relate to as making sense for soldiers. It tested your ability to sprint, change direction, and avoid obstacles. Come to think of it, those skills were handy on occasion during my adolescence on the streets of the north side of Chicago.

The last event was the run, which was either one or two miles. It was one mile for basic training, and two after that. Both were done on a quarter-mile track wearing a number stenciled on a piece of canvas. The whole test was done in fatigues and combat boots.

I played a lot of sports in my units during the next few years after basic training. Organized physical fitness training just didn't occur in those units. It was a fault of the type of units I was assigned to, I suppose—headquarters and garrison units. Or maybe it was standard for that time in the army. Unfortunately, it's still a problem in some units today.

From 1972 to 1977, I recall taking one PT test. The units I was assigned to just never had them. There were many pencil-whipped PT scorecards in those units. I never filled out a card without taking a test, but one always materialized when it was time to clear the unit.

The one test I took was one of the several versions of the test we had in those days. I took it when I was assigned to the 142d Military Police Company in Yongsan, Korea. I believe it was called the inclement weather test. We took it inside the gym, even though the weather outside was fine. If I remember correctly, we did push-ups, sit-ups, the bend and reach (do a hundred of those really fast, then stand up straight), the squat thrust, and something called the 80-meter shuttle run (you'd have to see it).

Lots of folks pencil-whipped that test right there in the gym. "How many squat thrusts can you do? 'Bout fifty?

OK." For the first few years that I was in the army, that was my experience with physical fitness. A lot of folks—leaders, actually—just didn't take it seriously.

In January of 1977, I reported to Gannon University in balmy Erie, Pennsylvania, during a blizzard of historical proportions. I worked very closely with a captain there. I credit him with shaping my philosophy on physical fitness. He taught me about strength training, endurance training, complex carbohydrates, and new words like *aerobic* and *anaerobic*. I learned about the importance of consistent physical fitness training that had some purpose other than to gratify a ranting drill sergeant or pass a fitness test.

That was also the first place where I learned to disassociate physical training from punishment. Think about that for a minute. In organized sports, what happened to you whenever you made a mistake? You ran laps, did push-ups or belly-flops, duck-walked, or hit the blocking sled. Just when all that was behind you, the army came along, and every time you screwed up a little, what happened? Push-ups, laps around the company area, whistle drills, and so forth. It was punishment. People don't like punishment. If physical training is used as a punishment, what do you think the long-term effect might be?

Anyway, back at Gannon I learned that physical fitness could be pleasant and that being in good condition felt a lot better than not being in condition. It was also necessary if you suffered from an affliction that both the captain and I had. Occasionally we liked to overdose on a thick-crust, double-cheese beast of a pizza from the South Erie Pizzeria. A six-mile run around the end of Presque Isle Peninsula was almost enough to offset one of those.

Gannon was the first place I ever ran that far without being chased by somebody.

Sometime during the 1970s, someone decided that running was the answer to all the fitness woes of the army. All of us were suddenly long-distance runners, like it or not. We had shoes, special shorts, and special shirts, and did all kinds of unusual contortions called stretching before we ran. Some folks got fanatical about it, and some soldiers got hurt trying to run marathon distances in combat boots to meet some standard pulled from who knows where. We had to meet that division standard, though—it was on the support form.

In drill sergeant school, unfortunately, I temporarily unlearned all that the captain had taught me about fitness principles. It was back to three conditioning drills and running in boots. The emphasis in drill sergeant school then was on learning how to teach and lead exercises, not on the physical fitness aspects of doing the exercises.

In the units, we still had drill sergeants who walked around with their hands on their hips correcting soldiers during PT. Sure, that was necessary during the first couple of weeks, and once in a while later, but we had guys and gals who did much correcting and little PT. Once again, we reinforced physical fitness as a punishment. I was just as guilty of it as anyone else. I did my PT, though, because, you see, I still liked pizza.

Today I'm not sure where we are with physical fitness training. We certainly have some things out of whack. We have convinced ourselves that it's such a complicated business, we have to send soldiers to a special school to become master fitness trainers.

On top of that, we have really screwed ourselves into the ground worrying over test scores and unit averages and other such nonsense. The obsession we have with getting 290s on our fitness tests has virtually destroyed the possibility of balanced fitness programs. Too many programs are nothing but practice for the three test events: timed sets of push-ups and sit-ups, and then a run. We may vary our positions for the push-ups and sit-ups and then run at whatever pace is good for us, but it still comes down to training for three events. It's not about total physical fitness. It's about a test score or a unit average.

I used to train hard for those test events. I trained my units the same way, because the score was everybody's measure of the worth of a fitness program. It's what commanders were and still are evaluated on. Over time, I relearned that a consistent, total-body fitness program is the way to go. The units for which I was responsible benefited from this approach. Our test scores and unit averages never dropped. The interesting thing is that we never had to cram for several weeks before the test. The test was just another day of PT, and usually a light one compared to the other days.

The point I'm trying hard to stress is that our test is not a measure of fitness, in my non-master-fitness-trained opinion. There are plenty of soldiers who can do well on the test and come up short on strength and endurance. Because you can run two miles in twelve minutes doesn't mean you can run three, four, or five miles anytime. Because you can do two minutes worth of push-ups and sit-ups (concentrating on your form so that they all count for the score) doesn't indicate that you can endure load bearing for an extended period. Because you can train a 135-pound body to do a bazillion push-ups doesn't mean you have the power to push away from someone who may outweigh you by 70 pounds.

We need to eliminate reliance on scores on a three-event test as our measure of fitness for individuals and units. Let's develop a test with pass-or-fail standards that measures a soldier's strength and endurance over a period of time—and I don't mean two minutes of this and two minutes of that and ten to fifteen minutes of running.

That's another issue. How many people actually use the entire two minutes for the strength events? Most are done in one or less. Those who are going to max the event do it in less than two minutes. Is there anything physical you can think of that a soldier might have to do that is done in two minutes?

Maybe I'm off target, not being a school-trained master fitness trainer, but soldiers need short bursts of speed and power and the endurance to bear a load over a long period. Why not measure strength by giving me a weight equal to my body weight and having me move it over a prescribed distance? If I can't shoulder and carry a weight equal to my body weight (representing a fellow soldier) for 50 to 100 yards, maybe I'm not strong enough. Test my ability to even lift my body weight, just once.

Two miles of running on a flat course is not much of a measure of anything. Most soldiers can trot that in sufficient time to pass the test. Let's have a five-mile course over varying terrain—which means some hills. Add to that some small obstacles that must be negotiated: ditches, wire, and so forth. Give me one hour to complete that course—in combat boots. When we have such a test, I think fitness will get back to being a total program and not a four-week crash course to prep for three events.

Coming up with a test that is a better measurement is only one step. Next must be the elimination of medical profiles that prohibit soldiers from being tested in certain events. I understand physical profiles. I have no problem with them. However, when we start making allowances that say one soldier has to do push-ups and one doesn't, one has to run and the other can walk, we have built an unfair system that applies different standards to doing the same job.

We need a baseline standard that all soldiers must be able to meet. The standard has to eliminate the possibility of profiling out of it. When the baseline standard cannot be met, then we have to seriously consider whether a soldier should stay in the army.

It has been nearly twenty years since we started seriously examining how we do physical fitness training, but not much has changed out where the rubber meets the road. There won't be much change, either, as long as we determine everything based on performance in a three-event test.

When was the last time you saw a unit playing spoke tag in place of their run? You do know what spoke tag is, don't you? When did you last see them do sprint relays, sandbag relays, quarter-mile interval training, or strength-and-aerobic circuits? When was the last time you saw them have fun and look physically tired after training? When was the last time you watched them do two minutes of push-ups and two minutes of sit-ups, jog two miles, look bored, and disguise that as physical training? The answers to those questions will be a better evaluation of your physical fitness programs than the unit's average score.

I know you may be thinking that you just received a sermon on PT. And you may not agree with the approach I've laid out. But if you are thinking about physical training and how it's done in your unit, then I have accomplished my goal. NCOs are the army's leaders on the physical training field. Physical training is as good as NCOs make it. Like everything else in a unit, physical training is a reflection of the NCO corps.

Chewin' the Fat

No discussion of physical fitness is complete unless followed by a discussion of weight control—or, more accurately, fat control. (Another sermon cometh.) Funny how we need a program to take up the slack where another program isn't getting the job done. For most things in the army, we need a backup plan. In this case, our backup plan is failing, and the price we're paying for it may be a little too high. I've seen the army's weight control program go from no control to out of control to too much control. We've turned what should be handled as a physical fitness problem into a bureaucratic management process. Too often, its end result is seeing good soldiers lost.

You may not believe this, but I had a drill sergeant in 1971 who was a monster in size. He was as big as a mountain, and it wasn't all muscle, I assure you. The odd thing was, none of the soldiers I was in training with thought that was strange. The man was a decorated combat veteran. He proudly wore a combat infantryman's badge (CIB) with a star on it. That'd be twice to war and back.

He was old and crusty and probably a little bit too fat, at least by current standards. We listened when he taught us something. It usually only took him one try to get most of us to understand things. Everything he taught us came with a sense of urgency in his voice.

While giving us extra marksmanship training in the company street, he let us know right up front that he thought the army had gotten rid of the best infantry weapon in the world and replaced it with "this little plastic piece of shit." He would go on to tell us, however, that if we learned what he taught us, "that we weren't going to get from those turds on the range," we just might be able to survive with this weapon anyway.

He told us things I have never forgotten. He gave us pointers that worked for me personally and that I have shared with soldiers for twenty-five years. "You keep that nonfiring leg (the left leg if you're right-handed) straight when you're in the prone position, and turn that toe in so it feels natural and comfortable. You take that firing leg, cock that knee a little bit, and let your toe point out. Not that way, shit fer brains." (And he'd go make some adjustment to somebody.)

"Now if you want to move your aim to the right or left, you cock that firing leg a little or you straighten it out a little. That gives you a natural point of aim. If you want to shoot a little lower, scrunch up and slide your belly forward a little without moving your elbows. If you want to shoot higher, slide your belly backward. It's that natural point of aim we're after, gentlemen, natural point of aim." There were many other tips like that, which you would never find in a book. They all worked. We listened and learned. Even trainees knew what a CIB with a star on it was.

I and many soldiers would not have had the benefit of this man's tutelage in today's army. Army Regulation (AR) 600-9 and someone's idea of what a soldier should look like would have pushed all that expertise and valuable practical experience right out the gate.

I watched this man walk for miles alongside us trainees. I watched him drag stragglers two at a time by their suspenders, telling them that stragglers die quickly in the jungle, or they get somebody else killed looking for them. No one ever questioned his physical abilities, but he would have been gone under AR 600-9 standards today. The army would have lost, and so would many soldiers, including me and the soldiers to whom I, and others I'm sure, transferred his knowledge.

Somewhere, in an honest attempt to look out for the physical health of soldiers, we got a little crazy with the program. Every day, the army loses productive soldiers who can meet the physical fitness standards but not the body fat standards. I still get brain cramps trying to figure out the logic of that. I have known way too many slender soldiers who didn't have the strength and stamina to go around the block unless their physically fit sergeants or buddies snatched them up by the suspenders and dragged them along.

How well the files are maintained and whether everyone has gotten their nutrition counseling before getting kicked out of the army measures the efficiency of unit weight control programs. If anyone ever sat down with a calculator and figured out the loss versus the gain and the cost to operate this program, it would probably be chucked in the trashcan tomorrow, or maybe even tonight.

Just bringing new soldiers into the army, training them, and sending them to their first duty station is an expensive process. Then we get them into a weight control program because they exceed the standard during a highly accurate tape test, which is the successor to the highly accurate pinch test. This causes someone to make a file consisting of about a dozen different forms and form letters for one soldier.

The commander's time is then spent counseling the soldier and providing him or her with the rules of the road. Appointments are made for nutrition counseling. A medical appointment is made to ensure there is no medical factor that precludes weight loss. The soldier is then put in unit special fitness training, which is not very effective in many units, and monitored for up to six months.

By the time the soldier meets the standard or is discharged, the file weighs more than the soldier does. A tremendous amount of time and resources are expended for what sometimes is about 1 percent of body fat. It might be cheaper for the army to offer liposuction. On top of that, a trained and possibly productive soldier, who likely has been performing a job up to standards, is gone. Soldiers travel across the world to schools, fail tape tests, and go right back to their units. That wastes money spent on travel and leaves us an empty school seat, another waste. It doesn't matter if the PT test was passed or not; flunk the tape test and you're out of here. Seems like an awful waste to me.

I guess I've done a lot of bellyaching here without giving any solution. The answer to the problem is simple. Step one: Throw the fat control regulation in the trashcan. Step two: Throw all the weight control files, the stats, and the silly damn tapes in the trashcan with it. Step three: Develop a tough physical fitness test that can't be passed unless you are in good physical condition—like the one I mentioned before—and that can't be avoided because of a medical profile. Make it a pass-or-fail test—no score. Step four: Have an unbiased committee appointed to do all fitness testing. Step five: Make the rules apply to everyone. Contrary to popular belief, they don't now. Get schools out of the PT testing business; send soldiers to school with physical fitness certifications from their installations.

There is no reason that we can't have physical fitness programs that keep soldiers fit and control their weight. The weight control program is just a stopgap that prevents the leadership from having to enforce participation in viable fitness programs. Let's get smart and use physical fitness as the tool to eliminate soldiers who are not physically capable of being soldiers or do not have the desire to stay fit. We sure aren't whipping them into shape with a fat control regulation. We can probably find enough wasted money in that program to bring back one of our divisions or renovate some soldier housing. Are you thinking?

Putting the sermon aside, just like fitness, fatness comes down to something very simple: NCO leadership. We have to work hard to keep good soldiers in the army, even if that means we have to take them out and run the crap out of them every night.

In one of my units, I required first-line leaders to accompany soldiers to special fitness training. One evening, I overheard a young sergeant tell a private, "You better hurry up and lose that weight. If it wasn't for you, I wouldn't have to be out here." You'll be pleased to know that I was very tactful when I explained to the young sergeant how he'd gotten that backward.

Every time I see a soldier hit the weight control program and have his or her career put in jeopardy, I see a leadership failure. Soldiers don't go home skinny one day and come back fat the next. A sergeant sees them every day.

Summary

- We owe it to the army to keep the best soldiers in it. We lose too many because of inadequate physical fitness training programs in units. NCOs are the leaders on the physical training field. We have to design fitness programs that stress soldiers and focus on total fitness, not passing three events on a physical training test. Fitness must be the focus.
- We can't afford to lose good, trained soldiers because we failed to run the fat off of them.

CHAPTER ELEVEN
FINAL THOUGHTS

Chickenship

I heard a story once. It was about a couple of neighbors. They were old retired folks living alone. One was an old man, the other an old woman. Both loved gardening and both were quite good at it. The old man, however, always had the most beautiful roses you could imagine. No matter how hard the old woman worked at her roses, they were never as good as his were. She tried very hard to find out what he was doing differently than she was, but never could. One day, out of frustration, she finally asked the old gentleman his secret. He walked into his garden shack and came back with a bucket. "Here's what I use," he said, as he passed her a bucket full of chicken droppings.

The old lady was surprised that he'd shared his secret with her. She was determined to have roses as good as his. Every couple of days she would go out and put a generous helping of the droppings on her roses. Soon, however, her roses began to droop over and die. Right away she accused the old man of lying to her. She told him that she had been putting the droppings on every couple of days and now, thanks to him, her roses were dead.

"There's your problem," said the old man. "You've used too much. Too much will cause them to quit growing; might even kill 'em. You just apply a little bit at the right time and they'll do fine."

Leadership is a lot like fertilizing roses. The right amount and type applied at the right time will get the job done. It will have a nurturing effect and allow those you are leading the opportunity to grow. Be careful about the amount you use. Because too much will cause them to quit growing; might even kill 'em. You don't want your leadership to turn into chickenship.

The Last Word

I have been writing down how I feel about things for many years. It's just something I do to help me think through things that are important to me and to those who have had to look to me for leadership. I never expected anything I had written to take on the form of a book. And certainly, I do not consider myself the how-to authority on NCO leadership. There is no one way to do it, and I've known too many great NCOs who were just better at it than I was.

My hope for this book is what I stated at the beginning: to add the NCO's voice to the discussion of leadership and generate discussion by NCOs about leadership. It's a voice that has been missing in a discussion previously reserved for officers. The noncommissioned officers of the army owe our thoughts on leading to the soldiers. The on-the-ground perspective is different from the bird's-eye view officers see. It's time to fill the void.

The real leaders of our army are noncommissioned officers: the men and women who, as a matter of their daily lives, lead, train, and care for soldiers and their families. There is no better way to understand leadership and what it entails than to witness, practice, and examine it in the three-meter zone.

NOTES